Assertiveness Training Programme for Teacher-trainees

Assertiveness Training Programme for Teacher-trainees

By

Dr. Sangeeta Pawar

Published, 2019

Published by

Gyan Publishing House
5, Ansari Road
Daryaganj, New Delhi-110002
Phone: 011-47034999, 9811692060
www.gyanbooks.com
E-mail: books@gyanbooks.com

Printed at: G. Print Process, Delhi.

Cataloging in Publication Data—DK
Courtesy: D.K. Agencies (P) Ltd. <docinfo@dkagencies.com>

Pawar, Sangeeta, author.
Assertiveness training programme for teacher trainess / by Dr. Sangeeta Pawar.
pages cm
Includes bibliographical references.
ISBN 9789386397980

1. Teachers—Training of—India. 2. Assertiveness training—India. I. Title.

LCC LB1727.I5P39 2018 | DDC 370.71154 23

Contents

Foreword

Teacher effectiveness is a major concern in the context of making our educative process fruitful and conducive to promote student-learning in a most desirable manner. The whole effort under teacher education is directed towards promoting this effectiveness. In teacher-training institutions the trainees are taught various skills that are considered to be important for communication of knowledge, building learning environment and helping students to move towards learning and understanding. Training for teaching involves selection of teaching unit, translating this unit in accordance to the previous knowledge of the student, selecting the approach for teaching the content, deciding upon progression of teaching in actual classroom, selecting the process of evaluation for testing understandings generated and practicing the knowledge attained through application etc. Preparation of 'lesson-plan' to organize teaching and then attempting to teach in accordance to various steps of the lesson-plan constitutes a significant practical component of teacher-training.

In actual conduction of teaching in classrooms, teachers interact with students in an ongoing situation in which they come face to face with students that have different backgrounds, understanding levels and potentials. These are living beings that have to be dealt with by teachers sometimes in a friendly manner with an empathetic understanding of their nature and orientations, while at others these need to be dealt with a firmness to coax them towards learning. Teachers are not expected to deal students in an aggressive manner, suppressing students and creating fear among them and thereby making learning process a mechanical one-directional transmission of knowledge. Nor are teachers expected to be submissive, being overly directed by the desires and requests of students. An assertive way of behaving in the classroom, based on appreciation of nature of students, their desires and potentials, letting students the opportunity to express themselves, appreciating students' and one's own rights in the ongoing interactive social situation, and being able to say 'no' when they want to say so, is the desired pattern in teaching-learning situations. To be able to do so in the classroom situation requires an optimal level of assertiveness among teachers themselves, and therefore it needs to be cultivated among student-teachers during the course of pre-service training. The study reported in this book exactly explores such a possibility through organizing an assertiveness training for student-teachers and testing its effectiveness. The study provides strong evidence that organization of such an assertiveness training in a workshop mode is conducive to this end. The author, Dr. Sangita Panwar, have undertaken a well designed research study, and on the basis of her findings she was able to point out policy implications for teacher educators as well as curriculum developers. It is expected that the book draws attention of all those who are directly involved in designing the format and curriculum of teacher education in the country.

Professor N.C.Dhoundiyal
Ex- Dean and Head
Faculty of Education
SSJ Kumaun University Campus
Almora-263601

Preface

A good personality can lead to be a good ideal among students. Assertiveness is generally accepted as most constructive method in communication and behaviour which facilitate the development of valuable personal qualities amongst individuals. Research in the area of assertiveness training recognize that these programmes have been introduced in various situations and lot of professional and social groups can get benefitted by becoming more assertive and adopting behaviours towards desirable direction. In present scenario, the teacher has to play multiple roles therefore the teachers will have to possess different specific skills including assertiveness. Application of assertiveness in teaching practice is said to increase the effectiveness of training activities and has positive impact among student-teachers.

The present book is the output of research and teaching experiences of the author. It is based on rich and updated review of works done in the field of assertiveness training and will help student-teachers to learn and acquire appropriate conversation and behaviour patterns for gaining professionalism in the workplace. The activities and exercises provided in the book will guide to organize appropriate assertiveness training programmes in training institutions for dwelling teachers as well as trainees in other professional programmes. The book is broadly divided into five chapters.

Chapter I devotes to understanding the background of assertiveness and assertiveness training. Definition of the terms viz., Assertiveness, Assertiveness Training Programme, Self-Acceptance, Academic Achievement Motivation and Female Teacher Trainees have been discussed in this chapter along with the Statement of the Problem. The chapter also covers Aims and Objectives, Significance and Delimitations of the study presented in the book.

Chapter II details the Assertiveness Training Studies in different Populations and outlines Studies on Assertiveness, Assertiveness across Individual's Characteristics and Correlation of Assertiveness with different Socio- psychological Characteristics. It further outlines the Discussion and Conclusions emerged through the Review of Research and discusses the Need to study the Impact of Assertiveness Training on Assertiveness, Self-Acceptance and Academic Achievement Motivation of Female Teacher-trainees. The chapter also details about the Hypotheses of the study.

Research Design is presented in Chapter III. The chapter highlights description of Population, Sample, Research Tools, Data Collection & Analysis Methods being used in Survey and Experimental stages of the study. A Test of Equivalence between Experimental and Control Groups and an Overview of Assertiveness Training Programme have been lucidly described in this chapter.

Chapter IV presents a Comparison of Level of Assertiveness among various Subgroups of Female Teacher-trainees. Comparison of Posttest Means on Assertiveness, Self- Acceptance and Academic Achievement Motivation among Female Teacher-trainees belonging to Control and Experimental groups, Comparison of Mean Gain scores on Assertiveness, Self-Acceptance and Academic Achievement Motivation among Teacher-trainees belonging to Control and Experimental Groups and a Comparison of Effect of Assertiveness Training on Posttest scores on Assertiveness within Sub- groups identified on the basis of Socio-demographic Characteristics have been illustrated in the Chapter.

Summary, Findings, Conclusions, Implications and, Limitations constitutes the subject-matter of Chapter V.

The book, it is hoped, will be useful for students, practitioners, policy makers, research scholars and teachers in the field of Teacher education. It will also serve as a sourcebook of activities for organizing assertiveness training for professionals in different training programmes. Suggestions are invited from all readers, experienced researchers and scholars for further improving the subject content as well as the presentation of the book.

Sangeeta Pawar

Acknowledgement

First of all I would like to thank God for his blessings that I become able to complete this endeavour. I feel short of words when, I take this opportunity to express my deep sense of gratitude and respect to Prof. V.R. Dhoundiyal, Faculty of Education, Kumaun University Campus, Almora and Prof. N.C. Dhoundiyal, former Head and Dean, Faculty of Education, Kumaun University Campus, Almora, who have a great influence on my academic and professional life. I am extremely grateful to the learned colleagues in the Department for providing me necessary stimulus for writing this book. I owe my sincere thanks and indebtedness to my parents and family members especially my husband Mr. Sachin Pawar and my children Harshita and Harshvardhan for their support and encouragement. I am grateful to all those persons whose writings and works have helped me in the preparation of this book. I thankfully acknowledge the assistance provided by the ICSSR, New Delhi in preparation of the manuscript of this book.

Sangeeta Pawar

List of Tables

List of Figures

Chapter - 1

Background of the Study

1.0.0 Introduction

> *"Teachers are the backbone of any country, the pillar upon which the aspirations of students are reconverted into realities. The teachers must be perpetual seekers of intellectual integrity and universal compassion"* — **Dr. Abdul Kalam**

The whole process of education is shaped and moulded by a human personality that is, the teacher who plays a pivotal role in any system of education. The American Commission on Teacher Education remarked that the quality of a nation depends on the quality of its citizens. The qualities of its citizens depend not exclusively but in critical measure upon the quality of their education. The quality of their education depends, more than upon any other single factor, upon the quality of their teachers". It is noted that teaching has been the largest, oldest and noblest profession. In spite of the technological advancements in the process of teaching learning, it has not been possible to replace the teacher. It is, therefore, not mere rhetoric to say that the teacher is the living ideal, the fountainhead of knowledge and the potential guide to provide direction for the growth and development of students, who are worthy citizens of tomorrow. In nutshell, teacher is the backbone of educational system, the maker of mankind and the architect of society (Rymbai, 2011). In the words of Dr. Abdul Kalam-"*I believe there is no other profession in the world that is more important* to society than that of a teacher".

Enlightened, emancipated and empowered teachers lead communities and nations in their march towards better and higher quality of life. They reveal and elaborate the secrets of attaining higher values in life and nurture empathy for the fellow beings. Teachers are the torch bearers in creating social cohesion, national integration and a learning society. They not only disseminate knowledge but also create and generate new knowledge. They are responsible for acculturating role of education. No nation can even marginally slacken its efforts in giving necessary professional inputs to its teachers and, along with that, due status to their profession.

Kothari Commission (1966) in its report observed that of all the factors that influence the quality of education, the quality, competence and character of teachers are undoubtedly most significant. The National Policy on Education (1986) has rightly remarked that no pupil can rise above the level of its teachers. The National Council of Teacher Education document (1998) has stressed that teachers are torch bearers in creating social cohesion and national integration by revealing and elaborating the secrets of attaining higher values in life. A teacher with sufficient competencies can render effective service and help in alround development of younger generations. In the context of present day realities, aims and objectives of education, a teacher is expected to perform multiple activities like teaching, evaluation, diagnosis of learning difficulties, providing remedial measures, organization of co-curricular activities etc, together with activities which are intrinsic to teaching and learning (Patri and Nanda, 2011). The teacher guides, understands, inspires, clarifies, facilitates, shares, serves as a role model, touches and transforms the life of a student with care and compassion. Thus, a teacher in the modern age, essentially require to be equipped with modern competencies to work effectively in order to cater to the needs of learners as well as the needs of modern society.

Teaching is a highly professional activity which demands specialized knowledge, skill and behaviour. Teacher professionalism comprises at least three essential characteristics: competence, performance and conduct, which reflect on teachers' personality and the way they behave in school and society. Competence is fundamental in teaching profession, which includes preparation of teachers for classroom processes and acquisition of knowledge of subject, and facilitates personality development of children. Competencies of an effective teacher include interpersonal communication, pedagogical empowerment and organizational leadership. Professional competence results in performance of teachers in terms of overall development of children. The competent teachers are expected to perform better in the interest of children and society. High level of competency empowers teachers with high selfconcept, commitment and motivational level. The third characteristic of teacher professionalism- conduct- is significant for a humane teacher, particularly in the Indian context. The manner in which the teacher conducts him/herself has impact on classroom, school, community and educational system. The teacher's conduct is reflected in the behaviour of young generation taught by him/her (Chaudhary, 2012).

Teaching as a social activity creates a dilemma for the person in this profession where on one hand he/she is faced with the requirement of satisfying his/her personal needs and desires, while on the other hand, people present around him/her expect him to fulfill roles, responsibilities/ behavioural patterns that they decide for him/her. The teacher has to remain in constant interaction with others. He is also required to deal with negative behaviours, like being criticized or forced to do some task, and maintain his emotional equilibrium. Needs of being able to identify one's own and others feelings, being able to communicate affectively and to manage one's own behaviours so that it remains socially acceptable, become significant for teachers. These and many other social skills are very important for developing healthy relationship with others and can affect many facets of a teacher's success in life.

On the part of various roles that a teacher has to play in his or her personal and professional life, assertiveness come up as a set of important skills to deal with a wide range of challenging situations, which demand expression of thoughts, feelings and beliefs in direct, honest and appropriate manner, standing up for personal rights while respecting the rights of others and as a process of social communication, involving exchange of thoughts and feelings, to establish satisfying social relationships.

Particular attention is being paid to the role of assertiveness in the modern educational system. Many authors have accepted assertive behaviour as the most constructive method of communication in teaching process. Its application in teaching practice not only increased the effectiveness of training activities, but also had a positive educational impact on young people, facilitating development of valuable personal qualities amongst them (Edwards, 2005; Nelsen et al., 2001). Implementation of pedagogical interaction of this type required specialized training in assertive techniques and skills by both teachers and students.

Assertiveness training is an area of study which has a long history with in the field of behaviour therapy. Ivan Pavlov in early twentieth-century demonstrated that behaviour brought on in the presence of one stimulus could be brought on by another stimulus if the second was paired with the first stimulus. He also determined that people behave adaptively to changing conditions in the environment. Pavlov introduced the concepts of excitatory and inhibiting forces and their interplay in learning and de-learning of behaviour (Fensterheim and Baer, 1978). Salter (1949) who founded modern behaviour therapy and Wolpe (1958) have recognized that certain individuals have specific problems in standing up for their rights and expressing themselves appropriately. These pioneers introduced the concept of providing assertiveness skills to help such individuals to function more effectively (Makhija & Singh, 2010), by making use of Pavlovian conceptions of excitation and inhibition as the basis for the treatment of nervous disorders. They stressed the need of a proper balance between excitatory and inhibitory processes in the brain for better psychological health. Since then the concept of assertiveness training has drawn the attention of many scholars, highlighting both its significance and making the term more precise. Lazarus (1973) influenced the development of cognitive therapy in the field of clinical psychology. Liberman (1975) introduced assertion or personal effectiveness training as a fundamental component of clinical services offered by community health centres.

Alberti and Emmons (2008), creators of the first assertive training intended not for clinical practice of psychological treatment of nerve disorders but for activation of human potential, emphasized that all people have equal rights regardless of their social status and believed that a sense of self-worth along with the assertive style of behaviour was not only desirable, but also necessary to be developed in everyone. They agreed that assertiveness was not a panacea against all troubles and failures that could occur in one's life, but through it, meeting challenges with confidence, the problems could be resolved in the best and adequate manner. The evidence established the effectiveness of structured learning and behaviour modification that occurs within groups. Assertiveness training is an important part of any form of behaviour therapy and based on the assumption that when any overt expressions of emotions are learned, displayed and reinforced, the corresponding subjective feelings will be felt (Anant, 2009).

Assertiveness training is based on the principle that we all have a right to express our thoughts, feelings and needs to others, as long as we do so in a respectful way. When we feel that we cannot express ourselves openly, we may become depressed, anxious or angry, and our sense of selfworth may suffer. Our relationships with other people are also likely to suffer because we may become resentful when others do not read our minds as we are not assertive enough to tell them. Assertive behaviour is specific to the particular time, situation, and cultural context. In other words, behaviour that is appropriately assertive for one person in one situation may be either excessively passive or too aggressive for someone else in a different situation.

Assertiveness training is based on the idea that assertiveness is not inborn, but is a learned behaviour. Behaving assertively can sometimes be difficult for almost anyone, and is often impossible for some people. For this reason, assertiveness training focuses on not only talking about the importance of assertiveness, but also on learning assertive behaviours and practicing these behaviours with the help of professionals. Assertiveness training aims to increase the number and the variety of situations in which assertive behaviour is possible, and attempts to decrease occasions of passive or aggressive behaviours (Hoffman 1983). Assertion techniques are tools for everyday life, enabling people to enhance their social contacts and become more effective in personal and professional spheres.

According to Smith (1985), in order to be assertive a human being not only ought to know his/her rights, but should be able to apply them in different situations and under different circumstances. Moreover, assertive training and compliance with assertive rights are important not only for the specific person (as means to realize his/her potential), but also for the society as a whole, as these would help to harmonize the social and labour relations. A detailed description of a training programme for group therapy, aiming to develop assertive skills in the communicative sphere, has been offered by Doty (1987). The necessary basic skills for the assertive training included the habits of dating and maintaining a conversation, skill of active listening, effectively dealing with conflict situations and ability to openly and adequately express feelings (both positive and negative) (Peneva & Mavrodieva, 2013).

Salter (1949) and Wolpe's (1958) emphasis on assertiveness skills was located in the field of behavior therapy, where individuals deficient in the ability to express themselves and stand up for their rights were provided certain skills during therapies. This approach seems to have later evolved into organization of assertiveness training programmes for individuals with special needs and for general students. Research activity under this approach typically involved selection of experimental and control groups, pre-testing these groups on assertiveness and some associated variables, introducing one or other form of assertiveness training and carrying out post-test in both the groups. The studies by Pitt and Roth (1978), Grant and Devorah (1980), Rotheram and Armstrong (1980), Hatzenbuehler and Schroeder (1982), Stewart and Lewis (1986), Lee and Crockett (1994), Firth (2001), Sert (2003), Lina, et. al. (2004), Flowers (2006), Tavakoli, et. al. (2009),

Makhija & Singh (2010), Agbakwuru & Stella (2012) and many others followed this approach. Many of these studies have noted that changes in assertiveness as a result of assertiveness training are also accompanied by changes in variables like self-esteem, self-concept, social skills, participation in different activities and academic achievement (Gangwar, 2012).

A large volume of research has been conducted on assertiveness training and these programmes are introduced in many settings. However, many of the assertiveness training studies were conducted on adults and some specific groups such as nursing staff (Gerry,1989 and Segal 2005); college students (Averett & Mc Manis,1977); students with learning disabilities (Firth,2001); indecisive students (Nota & Soresi,2003); working women (Brockway, 1976) and elderly people and adults with mental rctardation (Hatzenbuehler and Schroeder, 1982; Franzke, 1987 and Donnnelly, 1992).

With growing feminist attitudes in society during the 80s and 90s of the twentieth century (Castro, 1999) more attention has been paid to the role and rights of women. In response to the need for training of women in assertive skills and techniques, specialized training programmes for psychologists working with groups and tutorials for personal use were prepared (Heighway, et.al, 1992; Butler, 1992; Dickson, 1982; Goodman & Fallon, 1995; Leman, 1998; Shaevitz, 1999). Positive consequences of applying assertive techniques and acquiring assertive skills, authors indicated not only increased self-esteem, confidence and self-acceptance (Leman, 1998; Stake & Pearlman, 1980), but also reduction of emotional distress, depression, and general mental health (Butler, 1992; Chan, 1993; Pattenson & Burns, 1990).

In late twentieth century, use of assertiveness was more as a desirable aspect and it was used as a tool for self-development and self-improvement. In new millennium, this quality is being increasingly recognized as a prerequisite for employment in many professions, which are mainly related to communication. In early twenty-first century, assertiveness has become an integral part of professional relations in economic sphere, education, medicine, sports etc. Several specialized training programmes are being created for preparation of employees (Peneva & Mavrodieva, 2013).

To facilitate development of assertive skills among the professionals in educational system, certain programmes have been developed with the aim of increasing communicative culture, empathy, ability to self-control and emotions. Particular attention has been paid to the need of expressing respect for students and regarding their rights as fundamental characteristics of assertive behaviour (Savage & Savage, 2010). Application of these assertive techniques, according to specialists, affected the quality of teaching, improved self-esteem and personal satisfaction of teachers and led to lowering of occupational stress (Peneva & Mavrodieva, 2013). To build assertive skills in students, manuals containing guidelines for working with students of different age groups have been developed.

Mainly these recommended techniques to develop the ability to recognize one's own emotions and needs, to cope with negativity, to express positive feelings, to build respect and thoughtful attitude towards peers and elderly, and to raise self-esteem and self-acceptance (Christopher, Edwards, & Eppler, 2012; Kaufman, Raphael, & Espeland, 2000).

Special attention has also been paid to development of assertive skills among upper grade and college students, as it is believed that this age is conducive to build a vision, perseverance, self-reliance and initiative, qualities that are prerequisite for development of assertiveness (Peneva & Mavrodieva, 2013). This was implemented not only through specialized training and training programmes (Christopher, Edwards, & Eppler, 2012) but also through self-development, supported by tutorials for personal use.

Establishing effectiveness of assertiveness training in facilitating development of assertiveness and positive change in certain characteristics is one approach of understanding the phenomena associated with assertive behaviour and related aspects. Another, naturalistic approach, focused on surveying the level of assertiveness in a population of interest and attempting to analyze certain characteristics as input factors and others as dependent outcomes. Sex, age, social group membership, birth order, educational status etc. have been considered as input characteristics in shaping assertiveness, and similar to the experimental approach, selfesteem, self-concept, academic self efficacy and adjustment have been considered as outcomes (Gangwar, 2012).

The socio-demographic and cultural milieu in which a person lives and grows is an important factor in deciding whether he or she will develop into an aggressive person, submissive person or an assertive person. In Indian context, this socio-demographic and cultural milieu can be visualized as being shaped by factors associated with individuality, educational environment in which he finds himself and the socio-cultural environment produced by parental occupation and educational characteristics. The need to understand the role of socio-demographic and cultural milieu in development of assertive behavioural tendency is highlighted through the significance ascribed to assertive behaviour by different authors. (Gupta, et. al. (2002); Kaur and Mehta (2007); Noushad and Musthafa (2008); Makhija and Singh (2011); Gangwar (2012) and Asokan and Muthumanickam (2013).

On account of perceived benefits of assertiveness training programme in various fields, a need was felt to study the impact of providing training in assertiveness on various aspects of personality among prospective female teachers. Therefore, the investigator attempted to study the effectiveness of assertiveness training programme on personal and psychological characteristics of female teacher-trainees. These aspects seem to have not been explored in Indian situations and it is in this perspective that present study has been designed to explore certain background characteristics of pupil-teachers as input factors in shaping assertive behaviour, and impact of such kind of training on assertiveness, self acceptance and academic achievement motivation variables.

1.1.0 Statement of the Problem

In view of the perspective evolved in preceding section the problem of present study was stated in following words-

> "A Study of Effectiveness of Assertiveness training Programme on assertiveness, Self-acceptance and Academic Achievement Motivation of Female Teacher-trainees"

The problem of the study, as stated above, attempted to analyze the effect of assertiveness training programme on certain psychological characteristics of female teacher-trainees at B.Ed. level. These output characteristics included assertiveness, self-acceptance and academic achievement motivation among teacher-trainees. The basic assumption behind selection of these particular variables was the expectation that as assertiveness training programme are designed to raise an individual's self confidence and self–esteem, these will tend to impel trainees towards better acceptance of self and an increased motivation for achievement in academic field. The second aspect of the study envisaged survey of level of assertiveness among the selected group of teacher-trainees, and to analyze and compare this level of assertiveness across groups of trainees, identified on the basis of their selected socio-demographic and academic characteristics. This survey, analysis and comparison aspect of the study assumed that level of assertiveness among trainees is likely to be influenced by their background characteristics. Various background characteristics explored in this context, included socio-demographic characteristics like caste group, income group, father's occupational group, and parents' educational status, and academic characteristics like previous academic achievement of trainees.

1.2.0 Definition of the Terms

The statement of the problem of present study includes following key terms that need to be defined clearly.

1. Assertiveness
2. Assertiveness Training Programme
3. Self-Acceptance
4. Academic Achievement Motivation
5. Female Teacher Trainees

1.2.1 Assertiveness

Assertiveness has been defined in various terms by different authors. Lazarus (1971) stressed the idea of "emotional freedom" and described assertiveness as its subunit. He defined assertive behaviour as a 'social competence'. Jakubowski (1973) defined assertiveness as an act of protecting own human rights without violating the fundamental rights of others. Alberti and Emmons (1974) observed it as a behaviour that enables a person 'to act in his own best interest' and 'stand up for himself without undue anxiety'. It has been referred to as cognitive, emotional, and behavioural response that maximizes one's potential for reaching personal goals (Rich and Schroeder, 1976). Gervasio and Crawford (1989) have defined assertiveness as a style of conversation occurring in complex interpersonal context.

Wolpe (1990) defined assertiveness as 'socially justified motor or verbal expression of feelings'. Lizarrage, et. al. (2003) referred to assertiveness as an ability 'to express and advocate ideas, interest and feelings'. Noushad and Musthafa (2008) referred to it as 'courage to be oneself' and 'communicating honestly with family, friends and colleagues'. It has been characterized as an attitude of 'openness and receptiveness' by Anant (2009). Bishop (2010) defined assertiveness as the most constructive means of interpersonal interaction.

A covert assumption of respecting the needs of others by the person practicing assertiveness has been reflected by Makhija and Singh (2011). For Asokan and Muthumanickam (2013), acting assertively increases chances for honest relationships, feeling better about oneself and gaining sense of control in everyday situations. However, asserting oneself may not necessarily guarantee happiness or fair treatment. Nonetheless, by developing an ability to express, one is able to reduce stress, increase feelings of self-worth, improve decision-making abilities, and feel more self-confident in relationships. Assertiveness is the ability to reveal oneself overtly, straightforwardly and appropriately, to honour one's own feeling and thoughts as well as oneself and to discover one's own abilities and limits. Assertiveness is a behaviour that in addition to person's health increases the possibility of gaining pleasant results (Noghabaee and Nikoogoftar (2014). It has also been defined as way of communicating and behaving with others that helps a person to become more confident and aware of oneself (Tannous (2015).

An attempt to clarify the meaning of assertive behaviour through the identification of associated behaviours has been made by different researchers in the field. Thus, Lange and Jacubowski (1975) defined it as 'standing for personal rights, feelings and beliefs in direct, honest and appropriate ways, which respect the rights of the other people'. Galassi & Galassi (1979) referred to assertiveness as direct expression of one's feelings, preferences, needs or opinions in manner that is neither threatening nor punishing towards others.

Herzberger and Katz (1984) identified capability of free expression of emotions, ability to defend purposes or goals in general and specific situations as the components of assertive behaviour. Smith (1985) characterized assertive behaviour by mutual respect, benevolent perseverance and politeness. To Rees and Graham (1991), assertiveness means 'taking responsibility for life and choice', and 'making own decisions, rather than simply going along with other people's choices'. Okoli (2002) defined assertiveness as the proper expression of emotion other than anxiety, openness, directness, spontaneity and appropriateness.

In the view of Yong (2010), assertive persons 'resist undue social influence, disregard arbitrary authority figures and refuse to confirm to arbitrary group standards'. Hasanzadeh and Mahdinejad (2012) characterized assertiveness as speaking and acting with power, while maintaining respect for others. Instead of passively giving up power or aggressively demanding it, assertiveness enables youth to positively and authentically influence others. Not only confined to the freedom in expression of emotions, assertive behaviour, according to Abed (2015), demands control over outbursts of anger, crying or other behaviour patterns that exhibit lack of professionalism in the work sphere.

The above conceptualization of assertive behaviour has been summarized by Gangwar (2012) through listing behavioural tendencies that characterize assertiveness as follows:

1. Feeling free to express one's feelings and desires in various interpersonal situations.
2. Believing that one's feelings and desires are worthy.
3. Feeling free and able to make request.
4. Feeling free and able to refuse request.
5. Feeling free and able to defend one's opinions.
6. Feeling free and able to express feelings and desires in a direct and honest manner.
7. Feeling free and able to overcome pressures from others.
8. Feeling fearless in expressing one's desires and opinions.
9. Feeling free to do what one wants to do.

The above stated and similar behavioural tendencies in different interpersonal and social situations indicate presence of assertiveness in individual.

Assertiveness in present study referred to a variable measured by employing 'Assertive Behaviour Assessment Scale' (ABAS) developed by Dhoundiyal (2010) and re-standardized by the investigator for the teacher trainees at B.Ed.level.

1.2.2. Assertiveness Training Programme

Assertiveness training has been used in helping people to reduce their fear of acting appropriately in social and interpersonal situations. Assertiveness training techniques include broken records, fogging, free information, self-disclosure, negative assertion, transactional analysis, roleplaying and modeling (Okoli, 2002). Assertive training programme is a systemic approach to be more assertive in self-expression, based on a balance between achieving one's own goals and respecting the needs of others. It is a psychological intervention which helps participants learn to integrate assertive behaviour skills into their daily lives. It deals with attitudes, beliefs, and cognitions about assertiveness as well as specific overt assertive behaviours. The assertiveness training is based on the assumption that individuals do not behave assertively because they have not had the occasion to learn assertive responses in given situations, and aggression and non assertive behaviour are both learned response that can be replaced by an assertive response (Lin, et.al. 2004).

Assertiveness training is a life skill that causes an increase in selfesteem, rational stating of thoughts and feelings, anxiety reduction, improvement in social and relational skills, respecting other's right and increasing the rate of satisfaction from life and happiness (Hashemi, 2007). Iruloh & Amadi, (2008) added that assertive training is not therapeutic technique although it helps to teach an individual on how to assert himself despite the intimidation and pressures coming from other people. Furthermore, Corey (2009) explained that assertive training is based on the principle of social learning theory and incorporates many social skills training methods. He explained further that the training is often conducted in groups using modeling, role-play, and rehearsal to practice a new behaviour in the therapy office and then enacted in everyday life.

Assertiveness training has been defined by Zade, et.al. (2009) as a structural intervention which is used for social relationship improvement, anxiety disorder therapy and phobias in children, teenagers and adults. Assertiveness training is about acquiring learned skills and assertiveness training programme is designed to improve an individual's assertive beliefs and behaviours, which can help the individual change how they view themselves and establish self-confidence and interpersonal communication and subjective wellbeing (Paeezy, 2010). Akinteye (2012) opined that if well-taught, assertiveness training can help the person to recognize when they are being abused or maneuvered for someone else's benefit and how to resist such treatment effectively without becoming angry and aggressive.

It emphasizes the value of clear, calm, frank communication as a means of establishing relationships in which everyone knows where they stand and no-one feels ill-used. Yusefi, et.al. (2015) viewed that in assertiveness training an individual learns how to behave assertively. The person tries to solve and to define the problem, follows the aims assertively, repeats the roles effectively, changes them to form the pleasant behaviours constantly, and learns appropriate methods to express his/her wildlings assertively.

In the present study, assertiveness training programme referred to a specifically designed training programme adapted by Dhoundiyal (2005) in congruence with assertiveness skill training developed by Sue Bishop (1996) and includes the components of Self awareness, Awareness of rights, Refining goals, Nurturing self esteem, Feeling talk, Awareness of reasons of non-assertion, Ability to handle putdowns, Awareness of one's body language, Developing assertive body language, Being able to say 'No', Being able to make requests, Skill of handling conflicts, Ability to identify stereotypes and Handling discrepant situations.

1.2.3. Self-Acceptance

Self-acceptance is acceptance of self inspite of deficiencies. According to Shepard (1979), self-acceptance refers to an individual's satisfaction or happiness with himself, necessary for good mental health. Self-acceptance involves self understanding, a realistic, albeit subjective, awareness of one's strengths and weaknesses. It results in an individual's feeling himself as unique and worthy. Branden (1995) viewed selfacceptance to be the second pillar of self-esteem. The first steps of healing and growth, according to him, are awareness and acceptance consciousness and integration. In clinical psychology and positive psychology, self-acceptance is considered the prerequisite for change to occur. It can be achieved by stopping criticizing and solving defects of one's self, and then accepting them to be existing within one's self. That is, tolerating oneself' to be imperfect in some parts.

In present study, self- acceptance was operationalized as indicated by scores obtained on, 'Self Acceptance Inventory' (KSAI) developed by Kakkar (2010).

1.2.4. Academic Achievement Motivation

Achievement motivation commonly known as n-achievement, refers to the behaviour of a person who strives to accomplish something, to do his best and to excel others in performance. Atkinson's theory of achievement motivation grew out of research initiated by Mc Clelland et.al. (1953), who viewed achievement motivation to be a drive that can be experimentally aroused, differs from person to person and is acquired. It is considered as an important determinant of aspiration, effort and persistence. Thus, it is defined as how well a person does in comparison with a given baseline (Gupta & Shagufta, 2007).

Academic achievement motivation has been broadly defined as, an academic drive, attitude toward learning, and enthusiasm for academic achievement. Academic drive involves measuring items such as work habits and scholastic expectations, and attitude toward learning involves students' opinion of classroom environment and self-efficacy in learning (Entwistle, 1968). Enthusiasm for academic achievement involves the degree to which students possess certain specific behavioural characteristics related to motivation (Hwang, 2002).

In the present study, academic achievement motivation has been operationalized to be represented by scores obtained on 'Academic Achievement Motivation Test' (AAMT), consisting of two categories of statements, one indicating achievement motivation and the other showing absence of such motivation, constructed by Sharma (2010).

1.2.5. Female Teacher-trainees

The teacher training set up in India has been construed as a hierarchical system, of grades, subdivided into different stages or levels. Training for nursery school teachers is envisaged to prepare teachers for teaching children up to 6 years of age. Elementary school teachers' training extends to cover preparation of teachers for teaching class 1st to 8th. Training for secondary school teachers is provided to develop necessary knowledge, skills and attitudes among the teachers to teach students of class 9th to 12th i.e. students at secondary and senior secondary levels. In addition to these, training for special school subjects has also been envisaged for teachers of language, physical education, art and sculpture.

The Post-graduate teacher education courses provide education facilities for the students as well as teachers in higher education. Following this broad classification of Indian teacher training set up, female teacher-trainees of present study refer to the female teacher-trainees pursuing B.Ed. course from various institutions of Kumaun University, Nainital.

1.3.0 Aims and Objectives of the Study

The proposed study broadly aimed to investigate the effect of assertiveness training programme on assertiveness, self-acceptance and academic achievement motivation of female teacher-trainees. This broad aim was, however, subdivided into following objectives:

1.3.0 To survey the level of assertiveness of female teachertrainees.

1.3.1 To analyse and compare level of assertiveness of female teacher-trainees across sub-groups identified on the basis of their personal and socio-demographic characteristics. This was further divided into following objectives :

(i) To analyze and compare caste wise groups of female teacher trainees on their level of assertiveness.

(ii) To analyze and compare income wise groups of female teacher- trainees on their level of assertiveness.

(iii) To analyze and compare groups of female teacher-trainees, identified on the basis of occupational background of their family, on the level of assertiveness.

(iv) To analyze and compare groups of female teacher-trainees identified on the basis of educational status of their family, on the level of assertiveness.

(v) To analyze and compare academic achievement wise groups of female teacher-trainees on their level of assertiveness.

1.3.2 To study the effect of a specifically designed assertiveness training programme on level of assertiveness of female teacher-trainees.

1.3.3 To study the effect of a specifically designed assertiveness training programme on level of self-acceptance of female teacher-trainees.

1.3.4 To study the effect of a specifically designed assertiveness training programme on level of academic achievement motivation of female teacher-trainees.

1.3.5 To explore the effect of assertiveness training on level of assertiveness in groups of female teacher-trainees identified on the basis of :

(i) Caste

(ii) Family income

(iii) Occupational background of family

(iv) Parent's educational status and v Academic achievement

1.4.0 Significance of the Present Study

The significance of present study is derived from the fact that it is an attempt to study effectiveness of a specifically designed assertiveness training programme in teacher-education settings. Many benefits of training in assertiveness have been listed by different authors. These include reduction in anxiety, being able to make decisions in life, expression of feelings and thoughts, increase in interpersonal competence, self confidence, self-esteem and perceived self control through assertiveness training.

Teachers at present need to be goal directed, to be active towards attainment of these goals, to be expressive of their feeling and desires, and to be able in building healthy relationships with others. In order to face their challenging roles, teachers are required to understand their true selves and feel happy about themselves, besides being internally motivated for educational progress. In order to make our teachers more efficient in facilitation of knowledge development, more competent in providing quality education, more comfortable within society and more effective in using their professional knowledge and skills, it is necessary for them to be more assertive and have a high level of self-acceptance and academic achievement motivation. Therefore, we need to understand this dimension of behaviour in more detail, particularly in different socio-cultural settings. It is needless to say that assertiveness has to be instilled in a conscious manner through teacher education programmes. The present study is an attempt in this direction.

Development of personality is an important aim inherent in the organization of formal teacher education programme. How this personality is to be developed and towards what ends this development is to be facilitated, is a decision taken by educational planners. Inherent in various curricular and co-curricular components of educational process, this personality pattern incorporates elements like openness, industriousness, optimism, goal-directedness, ability to share thoughts and feelings, knowing one's strengths and weaknesses and acting in ways to strengthen one's self-esteem and productivity. An assertive behaviour pattern seems to incorporate these desirable personality traits, and it can be safely proposed that an attempt to develop assertiveness needs to be explicitly incorporated in educational settings. Incorporation of an emphasis on assertiveness development in educational-process, however, needs to be preceded by an empirical verification of the positive effect of assertiveness training on assertiveness, self-acceptance and academic achievement motivation among prospective teachers. A test of these assumed positive relationship, is inherent in present study.

Researchers postulate that assertive behaviour is marked by openness and receptiveness but, in our Indian society female child tends to be rated as a lesser being, subjected to suppression and discrimination in all spheres since childhood and denied of opportunities for self development. In such situations, they are never able to recognize their own potential and worth, and it hampers their alround development, particularly their assertive skills. Assertive behaviour has been viewed as an essential communication strategy for women in pursuing equality. However, within Indian value system females usually retain a submissive role and do not assert themselves well.

In recent times, government and non-government organizations are keen for improving the status of girl child. Great emphasis has been laid on girls' education, placement, promotion and better career options, so that they can compete confidently and assertively with their male counterparts.

Girls today have come up firmly by expressing their ideas, feelings and thoughts emphatically, without being rude and unreasonable, without offending others and having open, direct, honest communication and an active orientation towards life (Kaur & Mehta, 2007).

Teachers, more specifically female teachers have a vital role to play in the area of enhancing assertive skills among students and this is possible only when they themselves possess assertive skills and abilities. Assertiveness would help them to function more effectively in their everyday lives in dealing with personal, social and professional relationships. A socially skilled teacher can easily reach personal success and happiness with his or her social interactions. In today's world, where teacher has to play multiple roles, viz. friend, philosopher, leader, guide, counsellor, administrator and social activist, they have to face different challenging situations demanding dynamism, openness, communication skills and receptiveness. Therefore, teachers will have to possess different and specific social skills, including assertiveness.

Since assertiveness covers a lot of different social skills component, it is useful to give such training to female teacher-trainees, since women are generally considered to be lacking in these set of abilities (Shepherd, 2006). Especially, female teacher-trainees should be prepared for different life situations through assertiveness training so that they may transfer their learning to the next generation. Female, teacher-trainees are required to learn a complex set of social skills to engage in effective, confident and mutually beneficial interaction with others also. Female teachers, being reported to be emotionally high intelligent (Thilagavathy, 2013), could become an effective medium to transfer these assertive skills to students, more specifically to female students at various educational levels. In addition, it is a very important and useful social skill that has a power to enhance the social relationships, academic success and personal development.

Assertiveness and self-acceptance have a lot of commonalities: both are necessary and important character traits to live a satisfactory life and have healthy relationships with other people. Academic achievement motivation is also important factor for academic success and personal development. Thus, a thorough investigation of the interaction between these variables can highlight the ways to uplift interaction skills and assertiveness levels among female teacher-trainees. It is a necessity to empower young teachers with the knowledge, understanding and skills to choose their own appropriate and effective patterns of behaviour.

1.5.0 Delimitations of the Study

The effectiveness of assertiveness training programme on assertiveness, self–acceptance and academic achievement motivation could have been tested in different settings and within different populations. Moreover, research involving study on the effect of assertiveness training programme on behaviour, with different psychological and academic characteristics have been spread over different population groups and socio-cultural settings as outcome variables. The selection of population or setting for the present study is based on convenience of researcher, availability of relevant tools, availability of resources and familiarity with the context. Similar factors also guided the delimitations of present study. The present study is, therefore, delimited in terms of the following:

1.5.1 Population under Study

Study of effectiveness of assertiveness training programme could have been taken in different population groups available within teacher education system. The pre-primary, primary or elementary teacher-trainees might be considered or it was equally possible to conduct the study in a population belonging to higher education teacher educators. However, the focus of the study was narrowed down to female teacher-trainees of B.Ed. level, considering ease of data collection among this group of teachertrainees and the typicality of the nature of training undergoing within the group of secondary level teacher-trainees.

1.5.2 Variables Included in this Study

A selected group of psychological characteristics viz. assertiveness, self-acceptance and academic achievement motivation were considered as dependent variables in analyzing the effect of assertiveness training programme in the present study. A different set of psycho-social characteristics could have been envisaged to find effectiveness of such a programme. A few may be identified as self-esteem, self-confidence, adjustment, anxiety, social skills, teaching effectiveness, teacher pupilrelationship, mental health and satisfaction with life. Some more personal, socio-demographic and academic variables could have been studied that impinge upon development of assertiveness among female teacher-trainees, including factors of age, marital status, nature of permanent residence, birth order, home environment, nature of family, number of members in the family, attitudes in home and society and academic stream etc. All these were not included in present study. The researcher included caste group, income group, father's occupational group, fathers' educational status, mothers' educational status and previous academic achievement as independent variables to study their role in the development of assertiveness. The study was, therefore, delimited on selected variables only and did not include a number of possible variables due to constraints of time and resources.

Chapter - 2

Review of Related Studies

2.0.0 Review of Related Study

Research in the area of assertiveness training has evolved a large volume of literature which is helpful in recognizing that these programmes have been introduced in many settings and lot of professional and social groups can benefit from becoming more assertive and adopting behaviours toward desirable directions. The researcher, in the present review, have attempted to highlight major trends in assertiveness training research and understand interaction of assertiveness training programme on various socio-psychological and socio-demographic variables, in order to facilitate development of suitable hypotheses for present study. These selected aspects are focused in following sections of present chapter.

2.1.0 Assertiveness Training Studies in different Populations

Development of assertiveness training programmes and testing their effectiveness in improving assertiveness and associated characteristics of the sample studied has been a major thrust area of research in assertiveness. A lot of research efforts, focused to investigate the effectiveness of assertiveness training on different groups of people, have been done across many settings. The benefits of assertiveness training have been recognized by the researchers and thus these were employed in many professional and social groups.

Chitenden (1942), for the first time, conducted a study on pre school children on developing and measuring assertiveness. Findings revealed that children in the experimental group showed significant increase in cooperative behaviour and decrease in aggressive behaviours.

Investigation of effectiveness of group assertiveness training on non assertive college students was conducted by Galassi, et. al.(1974). Significant differences were found between experimental and control groups on the College Self-Expression Scale (CSES), eye contact and assertive content after receiving 8-week training, including videotape modelling, video-peer trainer feedback, behavioural rehearsal, group support and bibliotheraphy. These results exhibited that assertiveness training in groups, using video-feedback, was very useful for college students.

Thoft (1977) used assertiveness training with both passive and aggressive 4th, 5th and 6th grade children. After receiving training, group leaders, children and their teachers reported examples of more assertive behaviours in social settings. Pitt and Roth (1978) have proposed a model for assertiveness training and designed structured exercises for development of assertive behaviour. These structured exercises were found to be effective in learning assertiveness. The study also showed that feelings and behaviour jointly play an important role in learning assertiveness skills. The effectiveness of an assertiveness training programme among high school students has been tested by Grant and Devorah (1980). The study revealed more assertive behaviour among high school adolescents after undergoing the training.

Kelly, et. al. (1980) examined interpersonal evaluation of assertive versus unassertive behaviour, including the differential evaluation of assertiveness exhibited by males and females, and derived implications for assertiveness training. Results indicated that assertive models were rated lower on measures of likeability than unassertive models. This study also revealed that assertive behaviour exhibited by females evaluated in more negative form in comparison to evaluation of similar behaviour by males.

An assessment of the effect of assertiveness training on students was done by Rotheram and Armstrong (1980). Self report measures of assertiveness were collected initially from eighty five, 9th and 12th grade students, who were thereafter provided training with specifically designed assertiveness development programme. After undergoing training, a significant increase in assertiveness was noted among the participants.

Marshall et. al. (1981) tested relative effectiveness of assertiveness training and anxiety reduction in the treatment of unassertiveness and social fear. The study revealed that assertiveness training leads to an increased level of assertion, while it does not lead to decrease in the level of social fear. The efficacy of assertiveness training was examined by Buell and

Snyder (1981) by comparing it to a structured interview empathic respond procedure and an activity control procedure. Fifty-four male children and adolescents, ranging from 8 to 18 years in age, who were identified as non-problematic, mildly problematic or moderately problematic with reference to school performance, classroom behaviour and interpersonal skills, participated in the study. The results obtained from role playing test strongly suggested that giving assertiveness training to children leads to acquisition of behaviours which are viewed as interpersonally effective and assertive. These effects persisted after treatment.

Hatzenbuehler and Schroeder (1982) compared 44 mental health outpatients on assertiveness training through skill, cognitive and cognitive skill procedures. The experimental groups evidenced significantly more assertive and effective responses on both refusal and behavioural change situations. Kazdin (1982) evaluated separate and combined effects of covert modeling and overt rehearsal as a means of developing assertive behaviour among non-assertive clients. It was found that behaviour rehearsal approaches lead to significant improvements in self-report, selfefficacy and behavioural measures of assertiveness. It was also evidenced that combined procedure was significantly more effective in developing assertive behaviour. These three approaches to assertiveness training in developing assertiveness among non-assertive clients continued to be studied by Kazdin and Mascitelli (1982) and they further revealed that behavioural approaches improve social skills, global assertiveness and overt behaviour. The self-instructional and homework practice approaches were found to create more positive effects than the behaviour rehearsal approaches in the study.An attempt to assess the impact of assertiveness training on 4th and 5th grade children was made by Rotheram, et. al.(1982).

Higher assertiveness was reported among students receiving assertion training. The students were also found to be initiating more contacts with teachers. In addition, teachers also reported higher academic achievement and higher popularity among students pertaining to classes that were given training in assertiveness.

Barbaree and Davis (1984) examined assertive behaviour, self expectations and self evaluations of assertive behaviour as correlates of self-reported depressive symptomatology among university women. Discrimination training was found to increase the effectiveness of assertive performance and self evaluation ratings for all subjects. Moreover, increased assertion due to training was revealed to be much greater for depressed subjects than for non-depressed subjects. Stewart and Lewis (1986) analyzed the effect of assertiveness training on assertive behaviour and self-esteem among male and female black students studying at high school level. The experimental approach used in the study revealed no significant effects of assertiveness training on students' self-esteem and assertiveness.

An assessment of the effect of assertiveness training on self-concept and academic achievement was carried out by Beaver (1987). Forty students, enrolled in a vocational nursing programme, were involved in experimental study. Findings obtained through analysis do not reveal any significant change in both self-concept and academic achievement after the intervention. Starke (1987) engaged physically disabled young adults for the purpose of enhancing their social skills and self-perception and tried to compare effectiveness of assertiveness training and discussion support group in this perspective. Assertiveness training was found be more effective in enhancing social skills. Assertiveness training courses emphasizing differences among assertiveness, aggression, self esteem, female and male socialization and the relationship between assertiveness and everyday problems were conducted by Crandall et.al. (1988). Findings in the study revealed that assertiveness training increased self esteem and self-actualization level of college students significantly, with effects enduring for one year.

An assertiveness training was developed for a group of 2nd and 3rd grade children by Tanner and Holliman (1988) to modify their aggressive behaviour. Twenty-four children were assigned to an assertiveness social skills training or an attention control group. Results acclaimed moderate increase in frequency of cooperative interaction and a decrease in physical aggression among children given assertiveness social skill training. Lee and Crockett (1994) conducted a study on sixty volunteer, Chinese speaking nurses of Taiwan. The volunteers were divided into experimental and control group, with their assertiveness and stress levels measured at pre and post test situations. The assertiveness training group was found to improve in assertiveness and showed lower levels of stress as compared to volunteers of control group.

Assessment of a cooperative-creative programme of assertive behaviour and self-concept among 3rd and 4th grade children was done by Landazabal (1999). In pretest-intervention-posttest design, it was found that game programme of assertive behaviour, helpful behaviour and selfconcept encourage children to cooperate, share and develop creative play.

Results indicated statistically significant impact of programme on selfconcept in relation to affective and sociability aspects. Significant decrease in passive behaviour was also revealed along with improvement in assertive behaviour in the study. A qualitative study to investigate the effect of assertiveness programme on locus of control among young adolescents with specific learning difficulties was conducted by Firth (2001). It was concluded that assertiveness development programme effectively increases assertiveness and internality of locus of control.

Gupta, et. al. (2002) examined the effect of different techniques of assertiveness training on student's self-concept. Results indicated improved level of self-concept among students in experimental group. Kim (2003) attempted to study the effects of assertiveness training on social skills and assertiveness of visually impaired adolescents. Results reported positive changes in both social skills and skills of assertiveness after the intervention.

Training in assertiveness was also reported to be effective among indecisive students by Nota and Soresi (2003). In an experimental approach, the study revealed that assertiveness training improves students' ability to gather information for making choices, and thus improved level of decision making and decreased level of discomfort in social situations. Sert (2003) developed an assertiveness training programme and explored its effect among 5th grade children's level of assertiveness and self esteem.

In an experimental design, control and experimental groups were compared on pretest and post test measures. It has been found that assertiveness training has significantly positive effects on assertiveness and moderately positive effects on self-esteem of children.

Evaluation of assertiveness training programme on nursing and medical students was focused by Lina, et. al. (2004). The study analyzed the effect of assertiveness training on assertiveness, self-esteem and interpersonal communication. Positive effect on assertiveness and selfesteem were shown by the students who underwent assertiveness training, whereas no significant effect was reported on satisfaction in interpersonal communication. Stake et.al. (2005) conducted an experiment on the effect of assertiveness training on self-esteem of adolescent girls. After providing assertiveness training, significant changes in self-esteem scores were found. Flowers (2006) tried to identify the relationship between goal clarity and assertive behaviour and the effect of assertiveness training by using Rathus Assertiveness Schedule (RAS) and a test of goal clarity. It was revealed that there exists a positive correlation between assertiveness and goal clarity. Results showed significant increase in both goal clarity and level of assertiveness after training in assertion. Findings of a semi experimental study on female pre-high school students, with the aim to survey the influence of assertiveness training on the rate of happiness of girls, showed that assertiveness training is effective in the context of happiness (Hashemi, 2007). A study on 40 female students, in experimental and control group in pretest and posttest design, conducted by Mansur (2007), concluded that training life skills has a significant effect on self-esteem, progress motivation, and social adaptability.

Ashouri (2008), working with the 32 high-school students in Iran, showed that therapeutic group centralized on self-assertion and assertiveness caused a reduction in aggression and increase in educational progress. In an experimental design approach, Rezan (2009) provided training in assertive behaviour to one hundred and forty middle school students. Findings after intervention showed that assertiveness training was beneficial for developing assertive behaviour among students.

Effects of assertiveness training and expressive writing on acculturative stress among international students, studying in an American university, were compared by Tavakoli, et. al. (2009). The study revealed that group oriented assertiveness training facilitated lowering of stress and was more favoured by students in comparison to expressive writing, which found to increase their homesickness and fear. Kashani and Bayat (2010) tested effectiveness of social skills assertiveness training on assertiveness and self-esteem of female students, in an Iranian setting, who were found to be less assertive at initial stage. Assertiveness training was found to be effective in improving assertiveness and self-esteem of less assertive and shy female students. Assertiveness training was found to improve social skills of even the isolates by Nnodum (2010). Forty eight students from primary schools were assigned to four experimental groups in a quasiexperimental research design. It was revealed that isolates became more participative in class discussion, more interactive and less anxious in sharing their ideas after receiving assertiveness training. Modeling in this study was found to be equally good in changing the behaviour of isolates towards desirable directions.

Makhija & Singh (2010), working in Indian settings, undertook a test of effectiveness of assertiveness training among the adolescents. Involving eighty boys and eighty girls, studying in 10th and 11th grades in the public school of Chhattisgarh, Makhija & Singh (2010) revealed that the experimentalgroup of students, after receiving training in assertiveness, developed higher level of self-esteem as compared to students of the control group, which did not receive any such training. The study also concluded that assertiveness training programme do not have significant effects on academic achievement of students. Similar findings related to the effect of assertiveness training on academic achievement were obtained among female secondary students in Iran by Paeezy, et. al. (2010).

Mousa,et.al. (2011) aimed to determine the effect of an assertiveness training programme on assertiveness skills and social interaction anxiety of individuals with schizophrenia. In a quasi experimental design, 62 male individuals with schizophrenia were subjected to study and control treatments. Patients in the study group received group training sessions on assertiveness skills. The results indicated no differential changes between the two groups. Positive effect of assertiveness training on improvement of resilience among early adolescents was shown by Agbakwuru and Stella (2012). Twentyfour students were investigated in an experimental design approach. Findings revealed more improvement on resilience among girls as compared to boys. Akbari,et.al. (2012), determined the efficacy of assertiveness training methods on self-esteem and general self-efficacy of female students in Iran. Pretest and posttest experimental group design and multivariate analysis of covariance (Moncova) was carried out to test the research hypotheses among three groups of 20 people each, two experimental and one control. Findings obtained through the study showed significant effect of assertiveness training on self-esteem and general self-efficacy, in addition to reducing disability and confusion, resolution of conflicts and development of ways to solve problems and decision making.

Assertiveness training was found to reduce level of test anxiety among girl students in a study carried out by Niusha, et.al. (2012). Thirty students with test anxiety were assigned to experimental and control group in a quasi-experimental research design, with pretest and posttest and follow-ups at two occasions. The results indicated significant decrease in the level of test anxiety among participants of experimental group.

Asrowi and Barida (2013), working with the high school students of Indonesia, examined effectiveness of assertiveness training on communication skills of low assertive students. The results of pre test post test experimental design revealed significant improvement in communication skills after receiving assertiveness training. Students in experimental group showed courage to express verbally without being afraid of mistakes and showed good friendship. The study concluded that schools should give more attention and guidance for students to develop assertiveness. An evaluation of effects of assertiveness training on social anxiety of university students was carried out by Babayi and Rahmati (2014). In a pretest-posttest randomized group design, 60 students were randomly assigned to experimental and control group. Results obtained through analysis of covariance showed significant reduction of social anxiety and its components (Fear of public speech, strangers, other's judgement, social isolation and expression of anxious symptoms) among subjects of experimental group. Makinde and Akinteye (2014) analysed effects of mentoring and assertiveness training on adolescents' self-esteem. With descriptive survey and quasi-experimental design, findings obtained through analysis of covariance revealed mentoring and assertiveness training to be efficacious in raising adolescents' self-esteem. The study recommended these two programmes to be adopted by managements of schools. In an another study conducted among Iranian high school female students, Noghabaee and Nikoogoftar (2014) obtained significant effect of assertiveness skills training on enhancing self-efficacy of participants in experimental group. The study concluded that students need to be supplied with certain skills and abilities, especially assertiveness and efficacy for better operation.

In a randomized controlled trial Tavakoli, et.al. (2014) examined the influence of assertiveness training on self-esteem among female high school students. Sixty students were randomly assigned to intervention and control groups. After undergoing assertiveness training for a period of four weeks, mean scores on self-esteem and assertiveness of experimental group showed significant increase immediately and even after two weeks of training.

Abed,et.al. (2015) aimed to assess the effect of assertiveness training on improving self-esteem of psychiatric nurses. In a quasi experimental design (one group pretest-posttest design) 30 nurses were divided into six groups and provided assertiveness training for eight sessions. The results showed statistically significant effect of the intervention programme on assertiveness skills and self-esteem. Abed, et.al. (2015) also obtained a significant and positive correlation between total assertiveness skills and total self-esteem scores. Assertive training and systematic desensitization were found to have significant effect on examination phobia of university students by Chinwe (2015). In this quasi experimental, pretest-posttest control group study, it was found that assertive training and systematic desensitization were significantly efficient in reducing examination phobia among students of experimental group.

Tannous (2015) investigated effectiveness of assertiveness training in improving self-esteem among ninth graders with low emotional-behaviour traits. Existence of statistical significant differences between experimental and control groups revealed that assertiveness training programme contributed to development of self esteem among members of the experimental group.

Teaching of self-assertiveness skills was found to have positive and significant effect on self-esteem of blind girl students by Yusefi (2015). In pretest-posttest control and experimental group design, significant effect of intervention programme was found on general and social aspects of selfesteem. However, no significant effect of teaching self-assertiveness on educational aspects of blind students was revealed through the study.

The research work reviewed above, broadly indicates that specifically designed training programmes are effective in improving social skills and behaviour. These programmes have also found to be beneficial in facilitating positive development in self-concept, self-esteem, happiness, educational progress and participation in social situations. However, further research is needed to examine still more socio-psychological outcomes of assertiveness training.

2.2.0 Studies on Assertiveness

In addition to test of effectiveness of assertiveness training in changing selected psychological and academic variables in experimental settings, studies have also attempted to understand assertiveness and related phenomena through adopting survey oriented correlational approach. Such studies also throw important light on the processes associated with development of assertiveness and its consequences for the individual. In following sections such studies have been reviewed to derive understanding for present study.

2.2.1 Study of Assertive Behaviour among Students

Assertiveness studies are common in specific age groups of students, adolescents and college level university students etc. Starting from the lower levels, sixth grade, male and female students were studied for assertiveness-achievement pattern by Hedrick and Chance (1977). Findings of the study indicated that prediction of less assertive achievement behaviour for females than males was feasible only among average-ability children. High school and intermediate level students were studied in assertive behaviour researches. Branaman (1979) studied junior college students and found significant difference between low assertive and high assertive groups in the level of facilitative test anxiety.

Greco,et.al. (1981) worked to modify Rathus Assertiveness Schedule (RAS) for early adolescents with a sample of 7th grade students. The 30-itemed Rathus Assertiveness Schedule was modified for seventh grade population using the method of peer ratings. Split-half reliability scores attained moderate to high acceptability. Correlation of Modified Rathus Assertiveness Schedule with peer ratings established validity in three of the four experimental populations. Michelson and Wood (1981) developed a children's assertive behaviour scale, which measured general and specific social skills. The scale was standardized, and subsequently recommended for use in research. Fourth and fifth grade students were focused by Wojnilower and Gross (1984) for the study of assertive behaviour and likeability. Results suggested that assertive behaviour is valued by elementary school students. Validation of Children's Assertive Behaviour Scale (CABS) for children's of this age group was focused by Hobbs & Walle (1985). The study examined relationships between sociometric indices and scores of 160 elementary school children on the Children's Assertive Behaviour Scale (CABS) for determination of differentiation power of the instrument on social competence among children.

Assertive behaviour and associated variables were studied in high school students by Mentes (2007). An analysis of data gathered from 1089 students on Rathus Assertiveness Inventory revealed no significant difference on assertiveness levels and possibility of becoming active athletes. A sample of 400 higher secondary female students was studied by Kaur and Mehta (2007), to understand the effect of assertiveness and selfconfidence upon patterns of reaction to frustration and adjustment. The study concluded that low self-confidence reported in girls was the result of poor self-concept developed and learnt by identification and imitation of social behaviour, and such type of conditioning imposed upon girl child has considerable and everlasting impact on assertive behaviour.

Noushad and Musthafa (2008) conducted a survey on a sample of 590 students of class 9th and showed that assertiveness of secondary school students needs improvement. Significant difference obtained on assertiveness between rural and urban pupils in the study, emphasized identification of factors causing locale difference in assertiveness of secondary students. It was also suggested that teachers can facilitate students to become assertive through modeling, encouragement and other strategies. Gangwar (2012) attempted to study curricular and co-curricular components of assertive behaviour among secondary level students. It was found that level of assertive behaviour among secondary school students is not a significant factor in shaping academic achievement and participation in co-curricular activities. Hasanzadeh and Mahdinejad (2012), while investigating the relationship between self-assertiveness and student's attitude towards school among 1st, 2nd and 3rd grades students obtained no significant correlation between the two variables. The relationship between self-control and assertiveness behaviour of 10th standard students was studied by Asokan and Muthumanickam (2013). A positive and significant relationship was obtained between these two variables, and suggested increase in assertiveness behaviour of students may increase their self control.

In a recent study, Ibrahim (2015) investigated assertiveness levels of high school seniors with different demographic characteristics. An analysis of data gathered from 312 students, studying at five different high schools, revealed significant differences on assertiveness levels of students studying at different schools. The study also concluded to organize social activities in schools so as to make students more expressive. University level students were sampled in numerous studies. Galassi, et. al. (1974) revealed that college students scoring low on a measure of assertiveness indicated negative self-evaluation, feelings of inferiority, tendency to be anxious of emotional support from others and excessive interpersonal anxiety, whereas students who scored high on assertiveness exhibited confident, expressive, spontaneous, well defended, achievement oriented and influencing behaviour.

Galassi & Galassi (1974) attempted to validate a measure of assertiveness for undergraduate students. College students were focused in the study by Nortan and Warnick (1976) and revealed that assertiveness measures were related to sub-constructs of communicator style. Assertiveness in the study was found to be highly correlated with measures of verbal intensity, talkativeness and good communicator style. Social consequences of assertion, aggression, passive aggression and submission, as well as situational and dispositional determinants, of male and female undergraduates' responses to form of requests were studied by Epstein (1980). Analyses of variance for compliance, anger and sympathy yielded significant effects for mode of request and for situation. Significant Mode of Request × Situation interactions indicated that assertion tended to produce positive social consequences in reasonable request situations.

Monroe, et. al. (1981) compared the performance of 146 undergraduates with different conceptual complexity on measures relevant to competent assertive behaviour. It was found in the study that students with high conceptual complexity demonstrated greater content knowledge, direct delivery skill and fewer negative self-statements. Moreover, females with high conceptual complexity were found to be more assertive in difficult situations. Students with high conceptual complexity were again found to be more assertive in extended interaction tests, expressed consideration of the needs of others and more flexibility in sex-role orientation. Lineberger and Calhoun (1983) observed significant differences in assertive responses of Black and White American undergraduates. Blacks were found to be scoring higher on assertiveness, while Whites made more requests in interpersonal interactions.

Undergraduate students from West Virginia University were studied by Kearney et. al. (1984) for analyzing items on Rathus Assertiveness Schedule and Personal Report of Communication Apprehension. Factor analysis of responses of 160 male and 144 female undergraduates on these two scales yielded five factors: apprehension about communicating in groups and meetings, apprehension in interpersonal contexts, apprehension in public speaking contexts, preventing others from taking advantage and contentiousness. Only one common factor, apprehension in interpersonal contexts, was shared by items from both scales. Female undergraduates with high and low assertion were studied by Delamater and McNamara (1985). Findings obtained through univariate analyses of variance revealed that high and low assertive females did not differ in their perceptions of assertive and unassertive behaviours displayed by a female confederate during task oriented, naturalistic interactions. Further, assertive behaviour was not devalued relative to unassertive behaviour by the respondents. Kern and Paquette (1992) investigated the importance of assertion and its effects on long term naturalistic relationships among female undergraduate roommates. It was found that higher levels of assertive behaviour was associated with perception of greater competency and likability among the subjects.

Male and female undergraduates were also sampled by Piccinin, et. al. (1998). Results showed that anxiety related to global assertiveness was related to high motivation but not to the quality of all criticism responses, when the impact of situational legitimacy and assertiveness-related anxiety/ discomfort was studied on motivation and ability to generate effective criticism responses. Rodriquez, et. al. (2001) focused on variables associated with assertiveness among female teacher trainees. The study concluded that assertiveness is strongly affected by age and ethnicity. Rathus Assertiveness Schedule used in the study, revealed that undergraduate women in college exhibited lower scores on positive assertiveness than older women and that Hispanic women had lower levels of assertiveness than Caucasian women.

Twenty-one to forty-seven year aged graduate students were studied by Poyrazli, et. al. (2002). Findings obtained in the study indicated that English proficiency, assertiveness and academic self-efficacy contributed uniquely to the variance in students' general adjustment level, while students' loneliness was predicted only by gender and assertiveness. Orr and Ochoa (2004) evaluated college students in public post-secondary institutions on comfort with assertive behaviours. The study revealed no significant differences between students with disabilities and students without disabilities in terms of their discomfort with assertive behaviours on the variables of overall assertiveness, verbal assertiveness and prosocial verbal skills. Dating competency and status in relation to assertiveness and misconceptions of assertion among university students of an average age of 21 years were explored by Scherbarth (2002). Results depicted that neither dating status nor gender is predictive of assertiveness. Yong (2010) assessed private university students on assertiveness and academic procrastination. A three-way analysis of variance revealed business students to be less assertive than engineering students, female students to be less assertive than male students and younger students to be less assertive than older students.

Undergraduate students of different vocational streams were sampled by Giivena (2010) to examine the relationship between level of assertiveness and problem-solving skills. Statistical techniques of t-test, ANOVA and Pearson's correlation coefficient were used in the study and revealed negative significant correlation between level of assertiveness and problem-solving scores, which implied that increase in assertiveness levels leads to increase in problem-solving skills. Assertiveness levels and problem-solving skills of the subjects in the study were not found to be affected significantly by variables of gender, age, department, level of satisfaction from department and perceived fathers' attitude. However, perceived achievement level and satisfaction from peer relationships were found to significantly influence assertiveness levels and problem-solving skills among the subjects.

Haladin, et.al. (2013) worked to analyze the level of assertiveness among 229 undergraduates of a public university in Malaysia. Responses on Rathus Assertiveness Survey (RAS) revealed high level of assertiveness. The study revealed that communicative competence does not influence the level of assertiveness among undergraduate students.

The above mentioned studies clearly indicate that researchers have explored various aspects of assertive behaviour in different settings of elementary, secondary and higher education. However, a major research effort has also been directed towards examining assertive behaviour within medical and nursing settings. This approach was exemplified by the study of Lavin (1990). Using a descriptive correlation design, Lavin (1990) obtained significant positive relationship between assertiveness, selfesteem and conflict management styles of collaboration and competition. A significant negative relationship was found between assertiveness and an accommodating conflict resolution style.

Kilkus (1993) studied a sample of 500 registered nurses to determine assertiveness levels in the population. It was revealed that majority of nurses possessed assertive behaviour and believed in themselves and their abilities. The study concluded that self-assertion generated by such beliefs will eventually lead to personal and professional empowerment. Changing levels of assertiveness in Irish nursing students' were studied by Begley and Glacken (2004). It was found that students' self reported assertiveness levels rose as they approached completion of their education programme. It was also suggested in the study that to function as effective, safe practitioners, registered nurses need to be assertive, and therefore, education in assertiveness should be an integral part of their preparation.

Mc Cartan (2006) compared four measures among nursing students. An analysis of results revealed positive relationship between scores on Semantic Differential and the Rathus Assertiveness Schedule. Karagozoglu et. al. (2007), while studying level of self esteem and assertiveness of final year Turkish university students, observed that nursing students had obtained highest scores on variables of self-esteem and assertiveness. Assertiveness levels of nursing students were also assessed by Deltsidou (2009). The statistical techniques of ANOVA and Pearson's Chi-square were used for comparing scores between semesters and it was indicated that assertiveness levels displayed by students increase slightly in advance semesters as compared to students of first-semester. The study also suggested to encourage assertive behaviour through learning methods. Factors affecting assertiveness among student nurses were explored by Ibrahim (2011). This study highlighted positive relationship between assertiveness and psychological empowerment. Introduction of specific courses for enhancing assertiveness skills among student nurses was recommended by the study.

An investigation of relationship between levels of assertiveness and peer pressure was carried out among nursing students by Arslan, et.al. (2013). Results obtained through the study indicated positive and significant correlation between assertiveness and peer pressure. Eldeeb et.al. (2014) aimed to assess assertiveness and stress levels among nursing students and revealed statistically significant positive correlation between assertiveness and stress levels. The study recommended introduction of specific courses for acquisition of assertiveness skills, including stress management and coping strategies in curricula.

2.2.2 Assertiveness Studies in different Populations

Assertiveness, has been studied in diverse categories of adults, particularly women. The early work by Rathus and Nevid (1977) on psychiatric patients, including neurotics, schizophrenics and patients with personality disorders, was to establish concurrent validity of 30-item assertiveness schedule. Findings of the study indicated high correlation between the scores obtained by patients on RAS with therapists' ratings of patients' assertiveness on semantic differential scales, defining a general assertiveness factor. Diagnostic group comparisons in the study showed that assertiveness was highest among patients diagnosed as manifesting personality disorders, particularly women. Lewinsohn et. al. (1980) analyzed correlation between assertive behaviour and depression among adults and noticed a negative correlation between the two. American students were compared with Caucasians for dimensions of assertiveness by Fukuyama and Greenfield (1983). The components of assertiveness, assessed on College Self-Expression Scale, revealed significant difference in the two culturally diverse groups. The study indicated lower levels of overall assertion in Asian-American sample in comparison to Caucasians.

College students, psychiatric patients and normal adults were examined by Heimberg, et. al. (1983), to study cognitive self-statement patterns in relation to self-reported assertiveness. It was revealed that nonassertive subjects reported higher frequency of negative self-statements than assertive subjects. Perceptions of black subjects towards assertive and passive behaviour across interpersonal situations was studied by Kean et al (1983), where 354 black male and female subjects were asked to view a professionally developed videotape of a black male or a black female behaving in such situations. The dependent variables were assessed through an interpersonal inventory. As perceived by the black subjects, assertive behaviour was found to be as more competent but less likable than passive behaviour in the results.

Delamater and McNamara (1985) analyzed social impact of assertiveness among female undergraduates with high and low assertion, and revealed that although assertiveness is perceived to be highly competent and skillful dimension of behaviour, it is also viewed as an unfavourable characteristic in interpersonal situations. The authors also discussed clinical implications of assertiveness training in the study. Psychiatric aide's perceptions of patient's assertive behaviour were evaluated and compared with reactions of college students by Dura and Beck (1986). It was observed that psychiatric aides' rated patients more favourably than college students in aggressive and to a lesser degree in the assertive scenes.

Gerry (1989) investigated assertive behaviour of trained nurses in general hospital settings. Trained nurses came up to be less assertive at work than in general life situations. Chinese American and Caucasian American women were studied on measures of assertiveness and social anxiety by Sue, et. al. (1990). The Chinese-American women were found to be as assertive as the Caucasian subjects on all behavioural measures, except on self-report measure of fear of negative evaluation, where Chinese-American women were found to be more apprehensive of social situations than Caucasians.

Niikura (1999) compared Japanese with Americans, Malaysians and Filipinos with respect to psychological process underlying Japanese assertive behavior. Less assertiveness for Japanese American was found in the study as compared to U.S. white-collar workers. Rodriquez et. al. (2001) searched for significant variables associated with assertiveness among Hispanic college women. The study identified no significant difference in level of assertiveness across groups based on age, marital status, birth order and prior history of counseling. However, significant differences were obtained in assertiveness level between groups based on academic classification and ethnicity.

Goldberg-Lillehoj and Spoth (2005) examined the relationship between assertiveness and alcohol use among rural adolescent. Findings of this study enriched the idea of including multidimensional assertiveness skill development as a prevention intervention among rural adolescents. Segal (2005) investigated the relationship between assertiveness, depression and social support among older nursing home residents and concluded that increasing assertiveness and health status may be more effective than providing only social support in order to control depression among these residents. Demographic factors affecting assertive and defensive behaviour in preschool children were studied by Weigel (2006). Results of multiple regression analyses indicated effects of ethnic identity, number of parents in home, age and sex. The most assertive children tended to be nonwhite/ black, older, male and from single-parent homes. Chibuike, et.al. (2013), focused on the role of locus of control on assertive behaviour of adolescent. Results obtained through the study of 80 participants on locus of control and assertiveness inventory revealed statistically significant influence of locus of control on assertive behaviour of adolescents. The study implied to have a check on locus of control in assertive training in order to improve in assertiveness.

Assertiveness among psychiatric patients was studied by Eisler, et. al.(1975). Studying a sample of 60 male 21-67 years old hospitalized psychiatric patients, Eisler, et. al. (1975) indicated that interpersonal behaviour in assertive situations varied as a function of social context. Relationship of depression and assertiveness among normal and depressed individuals was studied by Mueen, et. al. (2006). Results obtained through the study indicated highly significant relationship between depression and self-assertiveness. The study concluded that selfassertiveness is a positive trait and leads a person towards a healthy personality without any complexes and regrets.

2.3.0 Assertiveness across Individual's Characteristics

The present section of review embodies the studies undertaken to search for the causes of assertiveness in certain background characteristics, such as sex, age, marital status, income group, parents' occupational group, educational status of parents, birth-order, nature of permanent residence, type of school and social group membership.

2.3.1 Assertiveness and Gender

Gender is often viewed to be associated with assertiveness. A number of studies looking at gender and assertiveness in general population have reported mixed findings. Hedrick and Chance (1977), while studying sex differences in assertive achievement patterns, observed that prediction of less assertive achievement behaviour for females than males was supported only among average-ability children. However, highability females demonstrated a deficit only in the most assertive behaviour.

Hollandsworth and Wall (1977) studied four samples total of 294 male and 408 female students. Men revealed themselves to be more assertive in areas like dealing with supervisor and bosses, being more outspoken in expressing opinions and in taking initiative in making social contacts with members of opposite sex. On the other hand, women indicated themselves to be more assertive in areas like expression of love, affection and compliments, as well as expression of anger towards one's parents.

A discriminant analysis of male and female's responses on Rathus Assertiveness Schedule (RAS) was performed to investigate sex-related differences in assertiveness by Crassini, et. al.(1979). In the results, males were found to score higher than females in certain areas, while in other areas females tended to more assertive as compared to males. Pitcher and Meikle (1980) have identified significant difference between males and females in level of assertiveness, while studying variations in assertive response topography and in type and frequency of reported self-statements in positive and negative assertion situations. Life satisfaction and assertive behaviour in the elderly male and female individuals with the age 60 years and above were studied by Piggrem (1980). It was shown that within this age-range, men tended to be more assertive than women. Mcfall et al (1982) explored the nonverbal components in communication of assertiveness among male and female subjects. High assertiveness was found to be expressed through nonverbal use of different body parts. Findings were recommended for organizing assertiveness training.

Assertive behaviour among Black students was examined by Bell and Jackson (1984). The study noted a significant difference between male and female students' assertive behaviour when interacting with their teachers. The finding was attributed to the process of socialization by authors. Lowe and Storm (1986) indicated that assertiveness has been viewed as more competent and likable by women observers, whereas passive behaviour in female model was more liked by men observers in their ratings. Studying the effect of culture and gender on self reported assertive behaviour among Israeli Arab and Israeli Jewish students, Florian and Shurka (1987) obtained significant difference in certain factors related to behaviour in specific social situations.

Crawford (1988) interpreted effects of gender, age and social evaluation of assertion. Gender and age were found to be influencing perception of assertion by subjects. Further, it was also revealed that females tended to be more assertive in initiating interaction, giving negative feedback, complementing others and admitting persònal deficiencies.

Conducting research on assertion among males and females, Worell (2001) has also summarized that men and women tended to assert themselves in different manners and in different areas. Worell (2001) pointed out that females remain more concerned with balancing their needs with the needs of others and show greater mutuality in assertive behavior. Females also use positive assertion more frequently than males. On the other hand, Worell (2001) pointed out that males display negative assertion more frequently and use assertive behavior in expressing one's influence and power over others. An investigation of the effects of age and gender in shaping assertiveness among persons of 20 to 60 years of age in a Nigerian sample was carried out by Onyeizugbo (2003). The findings revealed that younger men reported themselves to be more assertive than younger women, while older women reported themselves to be more assertive than older men. It was concluded that assertiveness may increase with age in women.

Orr and Ochoa (2004), on analyzing level of comfort with assertive behaviour among male and female students of post secondary institutions, reported that as compared to female students male students were found to be more comfortable with assertive behaviours in terms of their overall assertiveness and their verbal assertiveness. On the other hand, assertiveness levels was not found to be significantly affected by gender in a study conducted among undergraduates students of different vocational courses by Giivena (2010). In this connection, significant difference was obtained on students' self assertiveness strength between girls and boys in a study conducted by Hasanzadeh and Mahdinejad (2012).

In reference to socio-economic status, males belonging to lower and middle SES were found to be more assertive by Mueen, et. al. (2006). Male students were also shown to be more assertive than females in the works of Weigel (2006); Herni and Fakhrurrozzi (2007); Mentes (2007); Yong (2010) and Asokan and Muthumanickam (2013). In contrast, no significant difference was obtained in the level of assertiveness of male and female students among Nigerian education majors in the study of Ekundayo (2010) and secondary school students of India by Noushad and Musthafa (2008); however, female secondary students showed a higher level of assertive behaviour in comparison to their male counterparts in the study of Gangwar (2012). Moreover in recent investigations in relation to assertiveness and gender carried out by Arslan, et.al. (2013) and Ibrahim (2015) among nursing and high school students respectively, revealed no statistically significant differences in the scores of assertiveness in relation to gender.

2.3.2 Assertiveness across different Socio-demographic Characteristics

A number of significant efforts have been made by researchers to explore the interaction of assertiveness with a number of other socio demographic characteristics. These characteristics were identified as age, marital and educational status of the individual, birthorder and membership of different social groups. Life satisfaction and assertive behaviour among elderly people was studied by Piggrem (1980). The results showed that age and marital status were not related to assertive behaviour.

In their study on Black and White undergraduate students, Lineberger and Calhoun (1983) observed that Black students tended to be more assertive and showed different behavioural pattern towards White students. Blacks were found to use Black English vernaculars more frequently with Blacks and more aggressive behaviours towards Whites. Educational status and age of professional nurses were considered as variables related to assertive behaviour by Kilkus (1993). On studying a sample of 500 nurses from Minnesota (USA), Kilkus (1993) revealed that with increasing age professional nurses became significantly less assertive. Again, it was also found in the study that nurses who were better educated were more assertive than nurses with lesser levels of education.

Herzberger, et. al. (1984) analyzed the multidimensional aspects of assertiveness encompassing human expression, overall behaviour, cognition and effect. It emerged through the study that behaviourally assertive individuals are able to express their emotions, defend their goals, and establish favourable interpersonal relationships, while both positive and negative emotions can be appropriately dealt by cognitively and effectively assertive individuals. The social impact of assertiveness upon deferentially assertive subjects was examined by Delamater and McNamara (1991). Results indicated that in live conflict situation, assertiveness is regarded less favourable on some dimensions of interpersonal attraction than unassertiveness. Yoshioka (2000) highlighted the impact of ethnicity among women from different ethnic backgrounds and evaluated level of assertiveness in fictitious situations. The results suggested that assertiveness may have culturally relative definitions associated with the values upheld by different societies.

Undergraduate teacher trainees were focussed by Rodriquez, et. al. (2001). The study revealed that factors such as age, marital status and birth order are not significant in shaping the level of assertiveness among Hispanic college women. Weigel (2006), while studying the effects of demographic factors among preschool students, noticed that social group membership (Black-White), age and number of parents present in home influence assertiveness in children. Higher level of assertiveness was found among Black, older and children from single parent homes.

Mueen, et. al. (2006) considered marital status, educational status and socio-economic status as important functions in development of assertiveness. The study tended that low education and low socio-economic status develops a person into less assertive individual. Married individuals, however, were found to be more assertive as compared to unmarried ones. Assertiveness level of students was found to be related with educational level of their mothers in a study conducted on Greek students by Patera and

Politymou (2008). Assertiveness levels of undergraduates of vocational courses was not found to be significantly affected by factors of age, department, level of satisfaction from department and perceived fathers' attitude by Giivena (2010). However, perceived achievement levels and satisfaction from peer relationships were found to significantly influence assertiveness levels among the subjects. In contrast to Mueen, et. al. (2006), Ekundayo (2010) identified that marital status is not a significant factor in shaping assertiveness. In addition, religious affiliation was also not found to be significantly associated with assertiveness. A positive relationship between income of family and assertiveness level of students was, however, found by Ibrahim (2011) in a sample of nursing students.

Gangwar (2012) in his study on secondary school students found that level of assertive behaviour is not influenced by grade, type of school, age, caste group membership, nature of residence, income group and educational status of parents. However, occupation carried out by father tended to influence students' level of assertive behaviour. Contrary to this, Ibrahim (2015) obtained positive relationship between educational level of parents and assertiveness scores among high school students, whereas, occupation carried out by parents did not seem to influence assertiveness level significantly. Rural students expressed higher level of assertiveness in the studies carried out by Noushad and Musthafa (2008) and Asokan and Muthumanickam (2013).

A thorough investigation of studies carried out in perspective of interaction of different socio-demographic characteristics on assertive behaviour, clearly indicates that in different settings, different factors operate in a specific ways. A need to explore the interaction between different socio-demographic factors and assertive behaviour in Indian settings has emerged through this review.

2.4.0 Correlation of Assertiveness with different Sociopsychological Characteristics

Relationship of assertiveness with a number of socio-psychological characteristics was studied by many investigators. For example, Eisler, et. al. (1975) indicated that interpersonal behaviour in assertive situations varied as a function of social context in a sample of psychiatric patients. Relationship between assertiveness and anxiety among college students was analyzed by Orenstein, et. al (1975). Scores obtained on Rathus Assertiveness Schedule (RAS) and a Trait Anxiety Inventory (TAI), revealed that assertiveness is negatively related with neuroticism, trait anxiety and interpersonal anxiety among both males and females. These findings suggested that one tends to become less anxious and neurotic with developing more assertiveness.

Galassi et.al. (1974), through the analysis of scores obtained on a self expression scale, indicated that college students scoring low on assertiveness related adjectives showed negative self-evaluation, feelings of inferiority, a tendency to be anxious of emotional support from others and excessive interpersonal anxiety. Students who scored high, on the other hand, were found to be confident, expressive, spontaneous, well defended, achievement oriented and influencive.

Norton and Warnick (1976), while studying assertiveness as a communication construct among 58 college students on the measures of Rathus Assertiveness Schedule (RAS), College Self Expression Scale (CSES) and a test of communication style, identified positive correlation between verbal intensity and good communication. Averett and Mc Manis (1977) reported that college students who scored low on both extroversion and assertiveness were rated low on self esteem, traits of poise, ascendancy and interpersonal adequacy but simultaneously rated high on traits of socialization, maturity, responsibility and intrapersonal structuring of values. In contrast, subjects scoring high on both extroversion and assertiveness were found to have opposite pattern of trait ratings.

Branaman (1979) obtained a significant difference in facilitative test anxiety between junior college students with high and low assertiveness. The study suggested that both assertiveness and facilitative test anxiety were found to facilitate better academic achievement. Social consequences of assertion, aggression, passive aggression and submission, as well as situational and dispositional determinants of male and female responses to form of requests, when studied by Epstein (1980), indicated that assertion tended to produce positive social consequences in reasonable request situations. Four types of assertive behaviour- Directiveness, Social Assertiveness, Defense of one's interests and Independence- were revealed to be independent of hostility and social desirability but were found to be positively correlated with self-esteem in the study conducted by Lorr and More (1980).

Deluty (1981) attempted to understand the adaptiveness of aggressive, assertive and submissive behavioural styles, among two hundred and twenty three male and female children, aged between 8 to 10 years, in relation to their self-esteem, popularity and peer ratings of behavioural adjustment. The results indicated a significant positive correlation between assertiveness and self-esteem, whereas a significant negative correlation was obtained between aggressiveness and peer rating of popularity.

Lobel (1981) identified significant differences between extroverts and introverts on the basis of assertiveness. In a study on personality correlates of assertive behaviour, Lobel (1981) found that extroverts behaved more assertively than introverts. Effects of conceptual complexity on assertive behaviour among undergraduate male and female students were explored by Monroe, et. al.(1981): high conceptual complexity students exhibited high content knowledge, better direct delivery skills and less frequent negative self statement. These students were found to express more consideration for the needs of others and were more flexible in sex role orientation. Critical analysis of nine scales, which sampled self report assessment of assertive behaviour, was presented by Beck and Heimberg (1983). Issues such as norms reliability, validity, social desirability and reading difficulty of these self-report scales of assertive behaviour were elaborated by these investigators. Heimberg, et. al. (1983) focused on the assertive behaviour of college students, psychiatric patients and normal adults. The study by Heimberg, et. al. (1983) reported that psychiatric patients were less assertive as compared to college students and normal adults. Laura and Rothblum (1984) investigated the frequency of college students' procrastination of academic tasks and reasons for procrastination behaviour. Findings of the study revealed significant positive correlation between fear of failure and lack of assertion. However, aversiveness was not found to correlate significantly with assertion.

Levin and Gross (1984) analyzed reactions to assertive and nonassertive behaviour by observers and concluded that assertive models were viewed more likable and more competent than nonassertive models. The study also implied that non assertive individuals more frequently adhere to negative self statements than assertive individuals. Lohr, et.al. (1984) examined the relationship between irrational beliefs and unassertiveness. The results showed that irrational beliefs were unrelated to self-reported assertion. Role play measures of assertion were, however, found to be related to total irrational belief scores and the subscales of Demand for Approval and Dependency.

An attempt to examine social skills components that precede the delivery of a skilled overt interpersonal response to men among women was made by Robinson and Calhoun (1984). Using a cognitive behavioural system approach to assertiveness, Robinson and Calhoun (1984) indicated that high and low assertive participants differ in their evaluation of consequences for response options. Moreover, correlation results obtained in the study were found to be supportive of cognitive behavioural system approach of assertion. A study of legitimacy of request and ability to handle request among assertive and nonassertive subjects was undertaken by Chiauzzi and Heimberg (1986). This study pointed out that relative to assertive subjects, nonassertive subjects were found to evaluate requests as more reasonable and rated themselves as less able to handle requests. Lavin (1990) aimed to determine the relationship between assertiveness and self-esteem among female nurses. Results supported a positive relation between the two variables. An attempt to examine relationship between assertiveness, academic self-efficacy and adjustment of male and female graduates of 21 to 47 years was made by Poyrazli, et. al. (2002). High assertive students came out to be academically more self efficacious and felt less lonely. No significant correlation between power motive and assertiveness was explored by Fodor, et.al. (2006), while comparing the reactions of men high and low in power motivation to a hypothetical candidate with assertive behavoiur.

Mueen, et. al. (2006) obtained highly significant relationship between depression and self-assertiveness in a study among normal and depressed individuals. Karagozoglu et. al. (2007) studied 372 final year university students and revealed a significant positive relation between self- esteem and assertiveness. Female students high in assertiveness expressed greater deviations of extra punitive reaction pattern to frustrating conditions, whereas less confident girls reported strong super ego and more exta punitive reaction pattern in similar conditions in a study by Kaur and Mehta (2007).

The effect of participation in sports on the level of assertiveness among high school students was tested by Mentes (2007).

This study concluded that participation in team sports tends to develop better assertiveness than participation in individual sports. Patera and Politymou (2008) revealed strong negative correlation between assertiveness and empathic concern as well as between assertiveness and personal distress in a sample of Greek students. Makhija and Singh (2011) analyzed emotional factors that tend to inhibit or enhance assertiveness. The findings obtained revealed that fear of rejection was consistently related to non-assertion in females. In addition, emotions associated with met emotional needs such as no fear of rejection, willingness to risk rejection and subject's ability to express a strongly held belief were found to enhance assertiveness. Hasanzadeh and Mahdinejad (2012), while investigating the relationship between self-assertiveness and students attitude towards school revealed no significant correlation between the two variables among high school students. An investigation of relationship between levels of assertiveness and peer pressure, carried out by Arslan, et.al. (2013), indicated positive and significant correlation between assertiveness and peer pressure of students.

Asokan and Muthumanickam (2013) examined the relationship between self control and assertiveness behaviour and revealed a positive and significant relationship between the two variables. The study inferred that an increase in assertiveness among students can increase their self control. Results obtained through analysis of effect of locus of control on level of assertiveness, revealed statistically significant influence of locus of control on assertive behaviour of adolescents in a study done by Chibuike, et.al. (2013). Eldeeb et.al. (2014), while assessing assertiveness and stress levels among nursing students, revealed statistically significant positive correlation between assertiveness and stress levels.

2.5.0 Discussion and Conclusions that emerged through present Review of research

The researcher has tried to include as many studies as possible on assertive behaviour and training that have significance for present study. This effort helped in identifying certain broad trends in the area of research on assertiveness training. These trends of findings may guide further researches in this area and a conceptual framework for present study could be derived from the related studies. The following conclusions seem to emerge through present review:

2.5.1 Dearth of Research in Assertiveness Training in Indian Settings

A thorough investigation of related review reveals that only a limited work has been done in this particular area of assertiveness and training in Indian settings. The investigator could succeeded in including only a few research studies (Gupta et.al. (2002); Kaur and Mehta (2007); Noushad and Musthafa (2008); Makhija and Singh (2010); Makhija and Singh (2011); Gangwar (2012) and Asokan and Muthumanickam (2013) in present review . This indicates a dearth of research effort in this area in Indian settings. It also puts an obvious need of initiating more research activity to understand assertiveness training outcomes in different populations of students and teachers in specific settings of Indian schools and university system, and also in social situations.

2.5.2 Assertiveness Training Impact on Socio-psychological Characteristics

Assertiveness training seems to bring forth a significant impact in development of assertiveness, social skills and behaviour among children, adolescents and some other populations. The present review pointed effectiveness of training programmes in development of self-concept, selfesteem, stress-reduction, decision making ability and happiness, goal clarity, progress motivation, participation in social situations, social adaptability with a reduction of social anxiety, improvement in communication skills and resilience. In educational settings, besides the positive effects, assertiveness training was found to have significant influence in reduction of examination phobia, text anxiety and increase in educational progress among students. However, this also highlights that further research is extremely needed to examine the impact of assertiveness training on still more educationally important socio-psychological factors.

2.5.3 Interaction between Assertiveness and Socio-demographic Characteristics

The present review indicates that certain socio-demographic factors, such as age, gender, marital status, educational and socio-economic status, social group membership and ethnicity have a potential effect on the nature and quality of assertive behaviour adopted by an individual. In this respect, it is significant to study caste group membership (General Caste, OBC, SC, and ST), parental occupation and educational status in shaping assertiveness in Indian contexts.

2.5.4 Consequences of Assertiveness Training

The consequences of assertiveness training as, highlighted in the present review, entail better self-concept, self-esteem, lowering stress, increase in decision making ability, goal clarity, progress motivation, skills in interpersonal situations, social adjustment, improvement in communication skills and resilience, reduction of examination phobia and test anxiety among students. The long term effects of assertiveness training on such factors seem to be unexplored. In the context of effect of assertiveness training on academic achievement findings are not consistent and need further investigation.

2.5.5 Potential Areas of Training in Assertiveness

The present review revealed that a sizeable amount of research work on assertiveness and training has been carried out among students in various age groups, at various educational levels and in different settings, such as nursing and other vocational courses. This emphasizes that there is a need of focused research with groups that are directly or indirectly linked to the quality of teaching and learning. One of such important group, i.e. the group of female teacher-trainees, has been focused in the present study.

2.6.0 Need to study the Impact of Assertiveness Training on Assertiveness, Self-Acceptance and Academic Achievement Motivation of Female Teacher-trainees

The present literature emphasized need to study the impact of assertiveness training on assertiveness, self-acceptance and academic achievement motivation of female teacher-trainees on the ground that this area still remains unexplored in Indian settings. The researcher was able to review only a single research on assertiveness among undergraduate female teacher-trainees by Rodriquez, et. al. (2001). As assertiveness training was found to be effective in enhancing the social competency and interpersonal adjustment in different populations, it is significant to study these benefits among prospective female teachers.

2.7.0 Hypotheses of the Present Study

It is well indicated in the review of related research that certain directional hypotheses can be made with reference to the effect of assertiveness training programme on socio-psychological characteristics of respondents. Directional hypotheses may also be stated with reference to interaction between assertiveness and socio-demographic characteristics of the sample studied. However, in the context of specific objectives of present study and to facilitate appropriate statistical testing, following hypotheses, framed in null form, were proposed to be tested.

2.7.1 There is no significant difference in level of assertiveness among sub-groups of female teacher-trainees identified on the basis of their personal and socio-demographic characteristics:

(i) Caste wise groups of female teacher-trainees do not differ in their level of assertiveness.

(ii) Income wise groups of female teacher-trainees do not differ in their level of assertiveness.

(iii) Groups of female teacher-trainees identified on the basis of occupational background of family do not differ in their level of assertiveness.

(iv) Groups of female teacher-trainees identified on the basis of educational status of parents do not differ in their level of assertiveness.

(v) Academic achievement wise groups of female teacher-trainees do not differ in their level of assertiveness.

2.7.2 There is no significant effect of assertiveness training on level of assertiveness of female teacher-trainees.

2.7.3 There is no significant effect of assertiveness training on level of self-acceptance of female teacher-trainees.

2.7.4 There is no significant effect of assertiveness training on level of academic achievement motivation of female teacher-trainees.

2.7.5 There is no significant differential effect of assertiveness training on level of assertiveness in groups of female teacher-trainees identified on the basis of:

(i) Caste

(ii) Family income

(iii) Occupational background of family

(iv) Parent's educational status, and

(v) Academic achievement

Chapter - 3

Method of Research

3.0.0 Research Design

The primary aim of present study was to ascertain the effect of a specifically designed assertiveness training programme on level of assertiveness, self acceptance and academic achievement motivation among female teacher-trainees, with a subsidiary objective of conducting a survey for examining level of assertiveness among female teacher-trainees and to analyze and compare this among different population subgroups identified on the basis of various personal and socio-demographic characteristics. Significant aspects of research methodology adopted to fulfill these aims and objectives are described in following sections. With reference to its stated research objectives present research was carried out in two stages, viz.

3.1 .0 The Survey Stage

3.2.0 The Experimental Stage

3.1.0 The Survey Stage

Survey research method was adopted in this stage to assess level of assertiveness among B.Ed. level female teacher-trainees, classified on the basis of their personal, socio-demographic and educational characteristics.

The details of methodological aspects like population, sampling technique, description of sample, tools for data collection, and analysis of data are presented in following subsections

3.1.1. Population of the Study

Female teacher-trainees of different B.Ed. training institutions affiliated to Kumaun University, Nainital, functioning as a state university of Uttarakhand, were envisaged to be the population of present study. The B.Ed. training institutions affiliated to Kumaun University, Nainital work under four different administrative setups-(i) the campus of the university, (ii) government colleges, (iii) government colleges, running B.Ed. course in self-financed mode, and (iv) self-financed institutions managed by private sector. In this manner, population of present study was located in four categories of B.Ed. training institutions. The investigator collected a list of total institutions running B.Ed. course in affiliation to Kumaun University, Nainital from the university office (See Appendix-6) and identified forty-seven B.Ed. institutions. In academic session 2012-13, a total number of three thousand and eight (3008) female-trainees were pursing B.Ed. course in these forty-seven training institutions. The institution wise distribution of population is given in Table 3.1.

Table 3.1: Institution-wise Distribution of Population

University Campus	Government Colleges	Government Self-financed Colleges	Private Colleges
57	62	557	2332
Total	3008		

3.1.2. Sampling Method

In view of the fact that population of study was spread over four categories of B.Ed. training institutions, Forty-seven (47) B.Ed. training institutions identified through university list were categorized into government and private institutions. The investigator then selected four institutions from each category in random manner to finally select eight institutions from which the sample was to be drawn. Category wise list of B.Ed. training institutions selected in this manner is given in Table 3.2.

Table 3.2: Category-wise List of B.Ed. Training Institutions Selected for the Purpose of Data Collection

S.No.	Type of Institution	Name of the Institution
1.	Government Institutions	I. Faculty of Education, Kumaun University, S.S.J. Campus, Almora II. M.B. Government P.G. College, Haldwani III. Radhey Hari Government P.G. College, Kashipur IV. H.N.B. Government P.G. College, Khatima
2.	Private Institutions	I. Sarswati Institute of Management and Technology, Rudrapur II. Presentation College of Teacher Education, Kathgodam III. Devbhoomi College of Education, Banbasa IV. L.B.S.S. College of Education, Jaspur

Within each of the selected B.Ed. training institution, seventy percent of female-trainees, from the total female teacher-trainees present on the day of data collection, were finally selected in a random manner to constitute a sample of four hundred teacher-trainees. Thus, sampling method adopted for present study was multistage random sampling method. However, only three hundred and ninety four trainees could be included in the final sample due to reasons such as incompletely filled-in questionnaires, questionnaires responded in a set pattern without actually reading the questions, questionnaire responded through marking two answer categories on the same question and questionnaire filled-in illegibly- factors that are beyond the control of researcher. Table 3.3 and Table 3.4 present selection of female teacher-trainees from government and private institutions respectively.

Table 3.3: Selection of Sample from Government Institutions

Government Institutions	Total number of Female trainees	Number of Female-trainees present on the day of data collection	Number of Female trainees selected
Faculty of Education, S.S.J. Campus, Almora	57	54	38
M.B. Government P.G. College, Haldwani	33	30	21
Radhey Hari Government P.G. College, Kashipur	69	65	44
H.N.B. Government P.G. College, Khatima	69	66	45
Total	228		148

Table 3.4: Selection of Sample from Private Institutions

Private Institutions	Total number of Femaletrainees	Number of Femaletrainees present on the day of data collection	Number of Femaletrainees selected
Sarswati Institute of Management and Technology, Rudrapur	125	121	84
Presentation College of Teacher Education, Kathgodam	80	77	54
Devbhoomi College of Education,Banbasa	83	79	55
L.B.S.S. College of Education, Jaspur	81	78	53
Total	369		246

The main characteristics of sample thus selected from government and private institutions are presented in section 3.1.3.

3.1.3. Main Characteristics of Sample selected for the Study:

The sample selected in above manner was analyzed with reference to type of institution, nature of permanent residence, marital status, age, caste composition, academic achievement and academic stream.

Educational status, income and occupational status of parents were also viewed as significant variables in analyzing the sample characteristics. Table 3.5, and related data in Figure 3.1, represents the distribution of respondents in accordance to the type of institution in which they were pursuing B.Ed. course.

Table 3.5: Distribution of Respondents in accordance to the Type of Institution

S.No.	Type of institution	Number of respondents (percentage)
1.	Government Institutions	148 (37.56)
2.	Private Institutions	246 (62.44)
Total		394 (100)

It may be observed from Table 3.5 and Figure 3.1, that the sample was selected from two main categories of institutions. Of the total 394 respondents selected in the sample, 62% were receiving training in institutions run by the management bodies, while about 38% of the respondents were under training in government institutions.

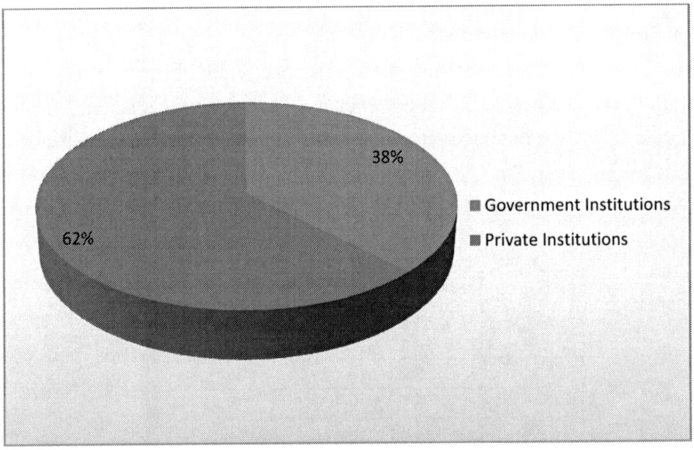

Figure 3.1: Percentages of Respondents from different Institutions

Distribution of respondents in accordance to the nature of their permanent residence is shown in Table 3.6 and Figure 3.2.

Table 3.6: Distribution of Respondents in accordance to nature of their Permanent Residence

S.No.	Nature of permanent residence	Frequency (percentage)
1.	Rural	162(41.1)
2.	Urban	232(58.9)
	Total	394(100)

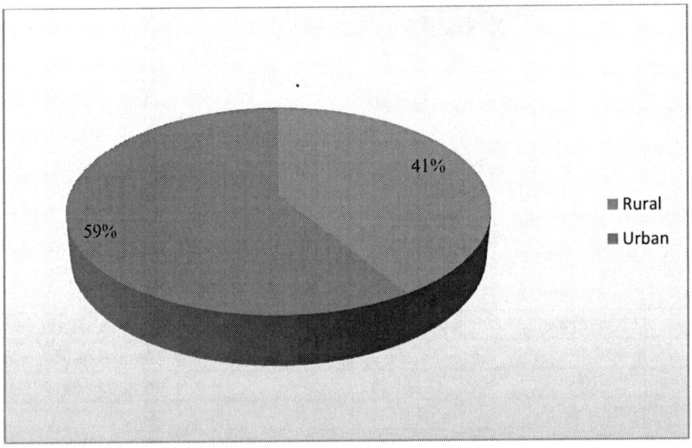

Figure 3.2: Distribution of Respondents in accordance to the nature of Permanent Residence

It may be observed from Table 3.6, and Figure 3.2, that about 59% respondents of the study belonged to urban areas and about 41% respondents belonged to rural areas. Table number 3.7, 3.8, 3.9 and related figures-3.3, 3.4 and 3.5 represents caste, age and marital status wise composition of the sample.

Table 3.7: Caste-wise distribution of Respondents selected in the Sample

S.No.	Caste group	Frequency (percentage)
1.	General	270(68.5)
2.	OBC	52 (13.2)
3.	SC	53(13.5)
4.	ST	19(4.8)
	Total	394(100)

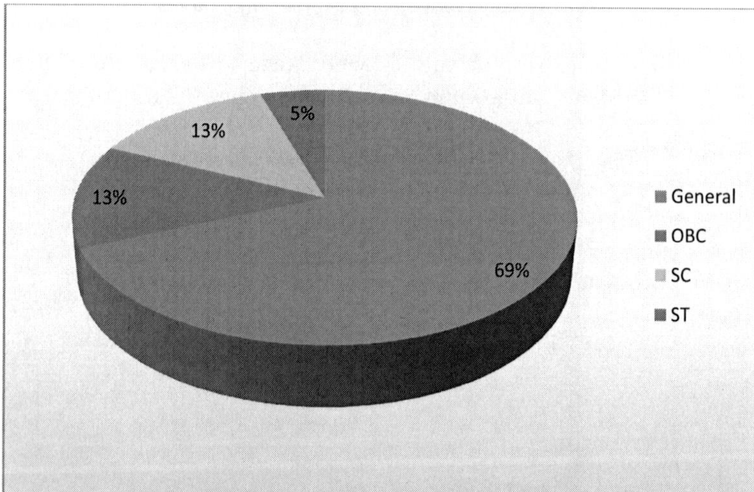

Figure 3.3: Caste-wise distribution of Respondents

Table 3.8: Age-wise distribution of Respondents selected in the Sample

S.No.	Age group	Frequency (percentage)	Statistical indices
1.	20-24	262 (66.5)	Mean = 24.5
2.	25-29	91 (23.1)	Median = 24.0
3.	30 & above	41 (10.4)	Mode = 22.0
	Total	394 (100)	SD = 3.5

Table 3.9: Marital group-wise distribution of Respondents selected in the Sample

S.No.	Marital group	Frequency (percentage)
1.	Unmarried	268 (68.0)
2.	Married	126 (32.0)
	Total	394(100)

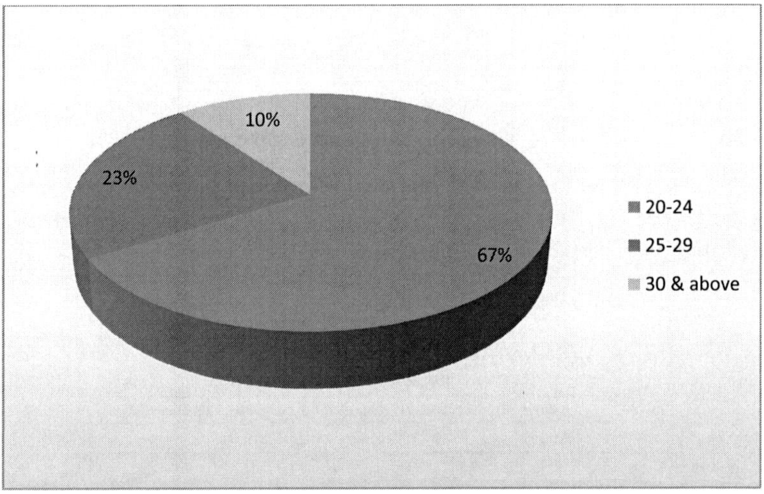

Figure 3.4: Distribution of Respondents in accordance to their Age

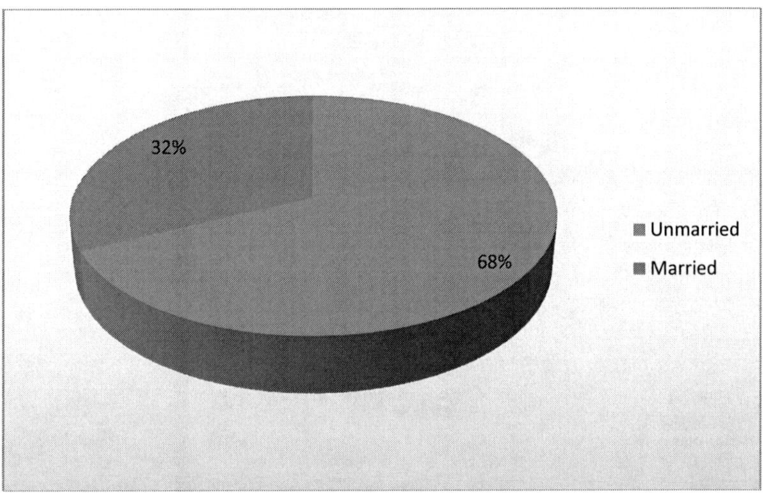

Figure 3.5: Distribution of Respondents in accordance to their Marital Status

An observation of Table 3.7 reveals that the majority of respondents, i.e. about 69%, belonged to general caste category, while other backward castes, schedule castes and schedule tribes respondents were represented by about 13%, 14% and about 5% respectively (See also, Fig.3.3). It may be observed from Table 3.8 and Figure 3.4, that majority of respondents (about 67%) belonged to the age group of 20-24 years, with a mean age of 24.5 years. The modal value of this distribution was 22 years, indicating that the distribution of age tended to be centered around this age value. Table 3.9 and Figure 3.5 indicated distribution of respondents in accordance to their marital status, and it may be observed that majority of them (68%) were unmarried, while 32% of them reported to be married.

Table 3.10 represents academic stream wise distribution of respondents and the related data is also shown in Fig-3.6. Academic achievement wise distribution of respondents is presented in Table 3.11 and Figure 3.7.

Table 3.10: Academic stream-wise distribution of Respondents selected in the Sample

S.No.	Academic Stream Group	Frequency (percentage)
1.	Arts	264 (67.0)
2.	Science	119 (30.2)
3.	Commerce	11 (2.8)
	Total	394(100)

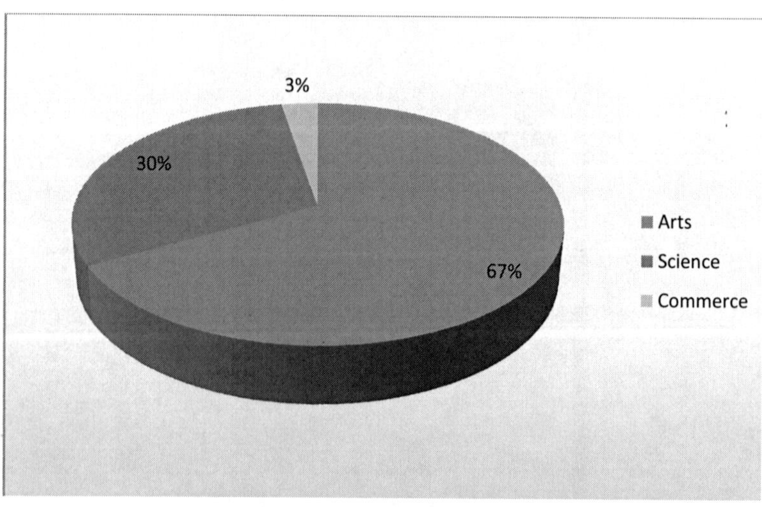

Figure 3.6: Academic Stream wise Mdistribution of Respondents

Table 3.11: Academic Achievement group-wise distribution of Respondents selected in the Sample

S.No.	Academic Achievement Group	Frequency (percentage)
1.	40-49	25 (6.3)
2.	50-59	265 (67.3)
3.	60-69	83 (21.1)
4.	70-79	21 (5.3)
	Total	394 (100)

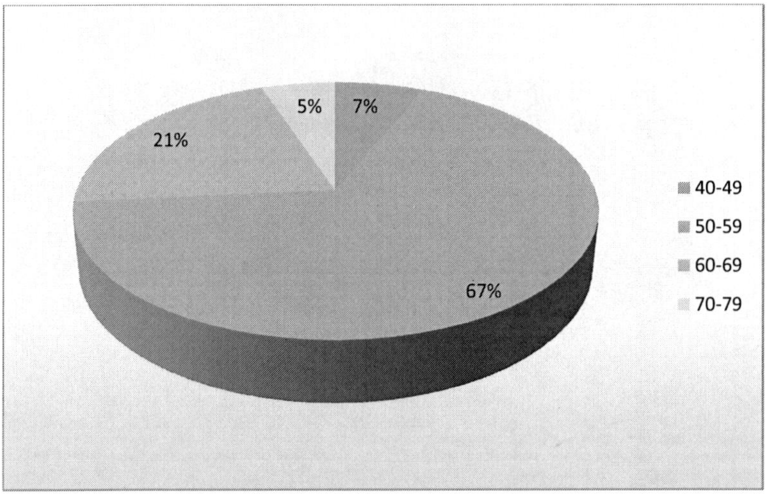

Figure 3.7: Distribution of Respondents according to their Academic Achievement Status

It may be observed from Tables-3.10 and 3.11 that 67% of respondents belonged to arts stream, whereas respondents belonging to science and commerce stream were about 30% and 3% respectively. It may also be observed that respondents obtaining 50 to 59 percent marks in the qualifying classes constituted the majority (about 67%) of the sample under study, while only about 5% were indicated to obtain marks ranging between 70 to 79 percent.

Table 3.12 represents father/ guardian's occupation wise distribution pattern of sample studied. This distribution is also presented in Figure 3.8.

Table 3.12: Father/ Guardian's Occupation-wise distribution of Respondents selected in the Study

S.No.	Occupational group	Frequency (percentage)
1.	Farming	53 (13.5)
2.	Teaching	44 (11.2)
3.	Government Employee	224 (56.9)
4.	Others	73 (18.5)
	Total	394(100)

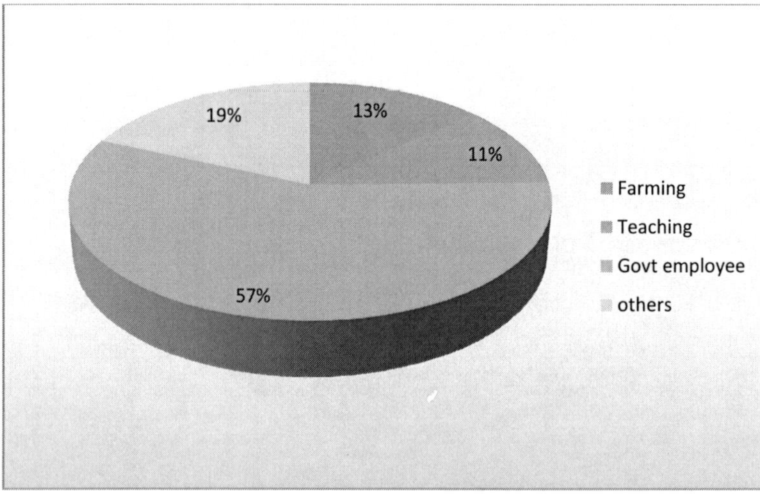

Figure 3.8: Father's Occupation wise distribution of Respondents

It may be observed from Table 3.12 that most of these respondents (about 57%) belonged to fathers/ guardians who were employed in one or other type of government organization. Fathers/ guardians of about 14% respondents were engaged in 'farming' activities as their primary occupation and fathers/ guardians of about 11% respondents were engaged in teaching works. Moreover, fathers/ guardians of about 19% respondents were reported to be engaged in other works, such as own business or working on daily wages as labourer.

Table 3.13 and Figure 3.9 present income group wise distribution of respondents of present study.

Table 3.13: Income group wise distribution of Respondents of the Study

S.No.	Income group	Frequency (percentage)	Statistical indices
1.	Up to10000	99 (25.1)	Mean = 17427.92
2.	11000-20000	81(45.9)	Median =15000
3.	21000-30000	65 (16.5)	Mode = 10000
4.	Above 31000	49 (12.4)	SD = 12748.54
Total		394 (100)	

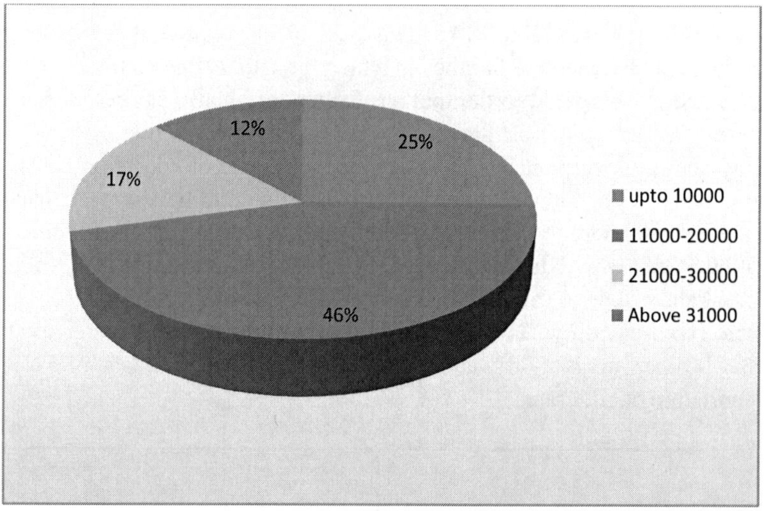

Figure 3.9: Distribution of Respondents in different Income groups

An observation of Table 3.13 and Figure 3.9 revealed that monthly income status of respondents' families ranged from Rs.10,000 and below to Rs.31,000 and above, with an average income of about Rs. 17,428/- per month. Minimum income recorded in the data was Rs. 700, while the maximum was at Rs.80,000/- per month. This distribution indicated large variation in the income status of families to which respondents of present study belonged.

Parent's educational status-wise distribution of respondents is shown in Table 3.14 and Figure 3.10.

Table 3.14: Parent's Educational Status-wise distribution of the Respondents of the Study

S.No.	Educational status category	Father's education, Frequency (percentage)	Mother's education, Frequency (percentage)
1.	Illiterate	7 (1.8)	44 (11.2)
2.	Primary	25 (6.3)	126 (32.0)
3.	Secondary	165 (41.9)	168 (42.6)
4.	Graduation	107 (27.2)	30 (7.6)
5.	Post graduation & Above	90 (22.8)	26 (6.6)
Total		394 (100)	394 (100)

It is indicated in Table 3.14 and Figure 3.10 that, in general, respondents of the study belonged to families in which the father was relatively better educated as compared to the mother. Fathers of about 23% respondents were educated up to post graduation and higher levels, while mothers of only about 7% respondents have attended this level of education. At the graduation level, fathers' representation was found to be about 27% and mothers just about 8%. It may also be observed that majority of mothers (about 43%) were educated up to secondary level as compared to about 42% fathers. A great variation was indicated at primary level where mothers were represented by 32%, while fathers were represented by only about 6% . Mothers of about 11% and fathers of about 2% respondents were also reported to be illiterate.

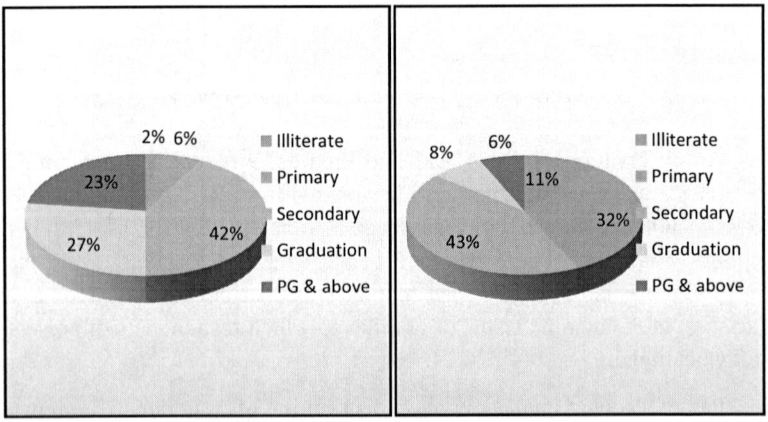

Figure 3.10: Distribution of Respondents belonging to Parents with different Educational Status

An analysis of socio-demographic and educational characteristics of respondents, shown in Tables-3.5 to 3.14, revealed that respondents of present study mostly belonged to general castes, were unmarried and residents of urban areas. Their mean age was 24.5 years, they belonged to arts stream and were second division holders in their previous academic achievement. These respondents belonged to fathers predominantly employed in government service and earning a mean monthly income of Rs. 17,428/-. Fathers of these respondents were quite often educated up to graduate level or above, while mothers of these respondents were more frequently educated up to secondary level.

3.1.4. Research Tools for Data Collection

Following research tools were employed for data collection in survey stage of present study:

- Personal Information Schedule.
- Assertive Behaviour Assessment Scale.
- Self-Acceptance Inventory (KSAI-K) developed by Kakkar (2010).
- Academic Achievement Motivation Test (AAMT) developed by Sharma (2010).

Description of above research tools is given in following subsections:

Personal Information Schedule

Following aims and objectives of present study, it was required to collect a number of personal, socio-demographic and academic information from each respondent included in the study. Therefore, a Personal Information Schedule was prepared by the researcher herself. The information requested in the schedule were mainly related to name, caste group, age, marital status, name of B.Ed. institution, nature of permanent residence, academic stream, percentage of marks obtained in final year's annual examination at graduation level, father's/ guardian's occupation, monthly income and educational status of parents. The qualitative information on these variables was obtained by asking respondents to either actually write the information or mark their response by selecting one of the categories provided in relation to specific questions. A total of 12 questions were framed to elicit information on these variables. The questions included in the schedule were framed in simple language. The respondents were also assured that the information provided by them will be kept confidential and will only be utilized for the purpose of present research work (Appendix-1).

Assertive Behaviour Assessment Scale

An assessment of assertiveness among female teacher-trainees at B.Ed. level in Indian settings was required in present study. Researchers had employed a number of research tools to carry out investigation on various aspects of assertive behaviour. For example, Rathus Assertiveness Schedule was used by Flowers (2006) and Rodriquez (2001), General Assertiveness Scale was used by Hernandez & Mauger (1980), while Mueen, et. al. (2006) used Self Assertiveness Scale. In present study, the investigator, however, attempted to standardize Qualitative Assertiveness Questionnaire, developed by Dhoundiyal (2005) for the teacher-trainees at B.Ed. level, through the process of pre-testing and undertaking reliability and validity analysis. The Assertive Behaviour Assessment Scale, standardized in this manner was used in present investigation (Appendix-2). The various steps adopted in standardization procedure are elaborated in following subsections.

- The initial pool of items.
- Screening of items with the help of experts.
- Re-Standardization of Assertive Behavior Assessment Scale.

The Initial Pool of Items

Assertive behaviour as operationalized by Dhoundiyal (2005), is the ability to express one's feelings and desire, ability to express one's thoughts and feelings in group situations, ability to say 'no' to unwanted demands made by others and ability to express one's likes and dislikes in various social situations. A qualitative assertiveness questionnaire was prepared by him, on the basis of this operational definition including sixtynine items which required respondents to indicate the frequency to which a particular behaviour pattern tends to be adopted by him/her in a specific social situation. The initial pool of items considered for development of present Assertive Behaviour Assessment Scale (ABAS) comprised of these 69 items. Here, it should be noted that these items were used by Dhoundiyal (2005) for sensitization of students of vocational courses in a specific department of Kumaun University, who were participants of an assertiveness training programme.

Screening of Items with the help of Experts

Two members of Faculty of Education were requested to scrutinized various items from the initial pool as considered above, in terms of suitability of language used for B.Ed. teacher trainees, structure of items, repetition of behavioural situations and relatedness of behaviours indicated in the items with the operational definition of concept of assertive behaviour.

A thorough scrutiny made by experts, identified all items to be directly related with the concept of assertive behaviour and structurally suitable in terms of language and complexity. These 69 items were then considered for inclusion in Assertive Behaviour Assessment Scale (ABAS). A Likert Type Questionnaire was prepared, in which both positive and negative items were present and each item was to be answered in terms of self-perceived frequency of behaviour arranged along five equal appearing response categories, which were given as always, frequently, indefinite, occasionally and never.

Standardization of Assertive Behaviour Assessment Scale (ABAS)

The Assertive Behaviour Assessment Scale (ABAS), developed through screening of items with the help of experts, was administered on a cluster of subjects selected (n=135) from the campus of Kumaun university. The responses obtained on different items were scored in accordance to positive or negative nature of items, so that a higher score indicated higher level of assertive behaviour. Scores obtained on each item by every student were entered into the data sheet of computer based statistical package for social sciences and this data sheet was processed through scale analysis menu for its reliability (Method Alpha). Items that contributed towards improving the alpha value through their deletion were successively deleted. In this manner a total of 12 items were deleted and a reliability coefficient of 0. 93 was obtained for the scale constituted of remaining 57 items. Table- 3.15 represents the results of reliability analysis conducted in this manner.

Table 3.15: Reliability Analysis of Assertive Behaviour Assessment Scale (ABAS) (ALPHA)

Item No.	Item	Corrected item- total correlation	Alpha if item deleted
1.	A01A	.39	.93
2.	A03A	.28	.93
3.	A05A	.35	.93
4.	A06A	.41	.93
5.	A07A	.40	.93
6.	A08A	.40	.93
7.	A10A	.36	.93
8.	A11A	.27	.93
9.	A12A	.28	.93
10.	A13A	.31	.93
11.	A14A	.29	.93

(*Contd...*)

12.	A15A	.28	.93
13.	A17A	.35	.93
14.	A18A	.42	.93
15.	A19A	.31	.93
16.	A20A	.25	.93
17.	A21A	.30	.93
18.	A22A	.46	.93
19.	A23A	.40	.93
20.	A24A	.39	.93
21.	A25A	.38	.93
22.	A26A	.47	.93
23.	A27A	.37	.93
24.	A28A	.32	.93
25.	A30A	.37	.93
26.	A31A	.50	.93
27.	A32A	.40	.93
28.	A33A	.44	.93
29.	A34A	.50	.93
30.	A36A	.53	.93
31.	A37A	.47	.93
32.	A38A	.55	.93
33.	A39A	.45	.93
34.	A40A	.42	.93
35.	A41A	.51	.93
36.	A42A	.54	.93
37.	A43A	.31	.93
38.	A44A	.55	.93
39.	A46A	.59	.92
40.	A47A	.49	.93
41.	A48A	.45	.93
42.	A51A	.52	.93
43.	A52A	.48	.93
44.	A53A	.45	.93
45.	A55A	.45	.93
46.	A56A	.49	.93
47.	A57A	.56	.93
48.	A59A	.31	.93
49.	A60A	.37	.93
50.	A61A	.44	.93
51.	A62A	.40	.93
52.	A63A	.55	.93
53.	A64A	.54	.93
54.	A66A	.28	.93
55.	A67A	.34	.93
56.	A68A	.44	.93
57.	A69A	.38	.93

In order to ascertain the validity of 57 items scale evolved in above manner, two criterion groups were identified by the investigator herself. As the member of Faculty of Education, it was convenient to select ten teacher-trainees, both male and female from two B.Ed. sections who showed assertive behaviour (expression of feelings and thoughts, initiation of interaction, participation in interaction, assertion of rights etc.) in day to day situations and ten other trainees who showed non-assertive- submissive behaviour (lack of expression of feelings and thoughts, lack of initiation of interaction, lack of assertion of rights etc.). Thus, a total of 20 students were identified by the investigator as assertive and non-assertive ones. The 57 item Assertive Behaviour Assessment Scale (ABAS) was administered on the trainees belonging to these two groups. Their responses were scored and mean and standard deviation values were compared. Table 3.16, 3.17 and related Fig-3.11 showed the results obtained.

Table 3.16: Comparison of Criterion group scores on Assertive Behaviour Assessment Scale (ABAS)

Assertiveness Groups	Number	Mean	Standard Deviation
Assertive	10	243.80	10.93
Non-assertive	10	175.40	12.49

Table 3.17: Results of ANOVA of scores on Assertive Behaviour Assessment Scale of Teacher-trainees of Criterion groups

Source of variance	Sum of	Degree of Squares	Mean freedom	Fvalue square	Significance at 0.05 level
Between Groups	23392.80	1 ·	23392.80	169.79	Significant
Within Groups	2480.00	18	137.78		
Total	25872.80	19			

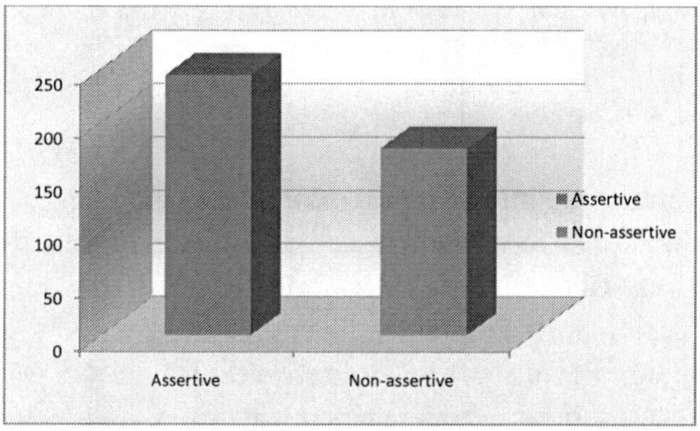

Figure 3.11: Mean scores obtained by Teacher-trainees of Assertive and Non-assertive groups on ABAS

Hence, Assertive Behaviour Assessment Scale (ABAS), developed as above, was found to distinguish pre-established criterion groups in a significant manner (F=169.79, significant at 0.05 level). This established the validity of Assertive Behaviour Assessment Scale (ABAS).

Self-Acceptance Inventory (KSAI-K)

In order to examine the self-acceptance level among respondents, Self Acceptance Inventory developed by Kakkar (2010), was used. It is a 34-item inventory that has been adapted from California Psychological Inventory.It is intended primarily for use among normal and sociallyfunctioning individuals of all age groups. The inventory covers a total set of 18 facets of personality, including self-acceptance that provides assessment of factors such as sense of personal worth and satisfaction with self. It has been standardized on 400 secondary teacher- trainees. It is a self-administering test that permits responses in "True-False" categories. Testing time is usually about 10 minutes. A high score of the individual on this inventory is indicative of intelligent, outspoken, short-willed, persuasive, verbally fluent, self-confident and self-assured personality, while those obtaining low scores are viewed as methodical, conservative, dependable, easygoing, quiet, self-abasing, passive in action and narrow in interests. The scoring procedure, according to the scale manual, is described in Table 3.18.

Table 3.18: Scoring Procedure for Self-Acceptance Inventory

Item no.	Correct response	Score provided
3, 6, 9, 10,11, 13, 15, 16, 19, 22, 23, 24, 25, 28, 30, 33, 34	'True'	'1' score for each correct response
1, 2, 4, 5, 7, 8, 12, 14, 17, 18, 20, 21, 26, 27, 29, 31, 32	'False'	As above
Total no. of item=34		

The maximum- minimum range of scores on inventory is 34. The sample for standardization was drawn from 1265 cases of stratified sample population. Test-Retest, Split-Half and Kudar Richardson reliability coefficients were reported to be .94, .94 and .77 respectively, and all were reported to be significant at .01 level. The validity of the tool was calculated by correlating test scores with an independent criterion measure of Teacher Quality for assessing self-acceptance, and it is indicated to be.79 (males) and .86 (females) significant at .01 level. (see Appendix-3).

Academic Achievement Motivation Test (AAMT)

A thirty-eight item, Academic Achievement Motivation Test, developed by Sharma (2010), was used to compare level of academic achievement motivation among the subjects of control and experimental groups before and after the intervention. The test provides a list of 38 statements, each having two alternatives, one indicating achievement motivation and the other showing absence of such motivation, the former to be assigned a score of one and the later a score of zero. The tool was standardized on 100 students (average age 14+), selected at random from schools of Patiala. The test can be administered to a group of not more than 40 students at a time. The usual time-limit is 10 minutes, though a few minutes more may be allowed where necessary. The numerical scores in the range of 0-38 are obtained according to the manual and the scoring procedure is described in Table 3.19.

Table 3.19: Scoring Procedure for Academic Achievement Motivation Test

Item no.	Correct response	Score provided
1, 3, 4, 6, 8, 10, 12, 13, 15, 16, 17, 18, 21, 25, 27, 31, 35, 36, 37	If box 'A' has been ticked	'1' mark for each correct response
2, 5, 7, 9, 11, 14, 19, 20, 22, 23, 24, 26, 28, 29, 30, 32, 33, 34, 38	If box 'B' has been ticked	As above
Total no. of item=38		

A score of thirty-three or above for boys and 34 or above for girls indicate high academic motivation. Average academic motivation in boys is indicated by scores between 26 to 32 and 27 to 33 in girls, while a score of 25 or below for boys and 26 or below for girls refer to low academic motivation. Split-Half and Test-Retest reliability of the test was measured to be .70 and .80 for boys and girls respectively. The criterion validity of the tool was established by comparing scores of two groups, one high in achievement motivation and the other low on achievement motivation as identified on the basis of judgements made by class teachers. Significant difference was found in the mean test-scores of the two groups (see Appendix-4).

3.1.5. Data Collection at Survey Stage

The x, development and printing of research tools needed for study, were followed by random selection of institutions for data collection.

The investigator visited selected eight institutions and with the permission of concerned Heads, met teacher-trainees of these institutions, who were explained the nature and purpose of questionnaires to be filled in by them. Only the female trainees were asked to fill the questionnaires. They were also instructed to answer various questions on the basis of their own feelings and not to consult their fellow trainees.

Female trainees were also asked to seek explanation of any word they felt difficult in understanding. The investigator promptly explained meaning of the word and/or sentence in simpler manner and through giving suitable xamples in some instances, whenever request for explanation was made by subjects. The data of survey stage were, thus, collected in a group situation, with a provision of providing individual help whenever required. The Personal Information Schedule was provided to trainees at first, for writing information demanded about themselves and their families. They were then supplied with Assertive Behaviour Assessment Scale, which required them to report the felt frequency of behaviour indicated by different items of the scale. Female teacher-trainees were later on provided with self-acceptance inventory and academic achievement motivation test. In general, respondents completed four research tools in 45 to 50 minutes. On the basis of procedures followed in data collection, it could be stated that investigator was able to collect data from respondents in a reliable and valid manner.

3.1.6. Method of Survey Data Analysis

Data obtained in survey stage were analyzed by making use of descriptive and inferential statistical methods. Under descriptive approach, frequency distribution, percentage analysis as well as calculation of mean and median values was undertaken to describe nature of distribution of different variables. However, one-way analysis of variance was carried out to find interaction between selected independent and dependent variables within inferential approach. Caste-group, income group, father's occupational group, parents' educational status and academic achievement of trainees were taken as independent variables in the analysis to find out their interaction with assertiveness among teacher trainees. Results obtained through this data analysis are presented and discussed in chapter on data analysis and interpretation.

3.2.0 The Experimental Stage

In this stage, experimental research method was adopted to assess the effect of assertiveness training programme on level of assertiveness, self- acceptance and academic achievement motivation among B.Ed. level female teacher-trainees. The methodological aspects like design, sample, sampling technique, intervention programme organization, tools of data collection and analysis of data are detailed in following subsections-

3.2.1 Description of Experimental Stage

Pretest-Posttest Equivalent-Groups Design was employed at this stage, where two B.Ed. teacher-training institutions from previously selected eight institutions (at stage I) affiliated to Kumaun University, Nainital were randomly selected for assigning to control and experimental group treatment. However, facilities such as: (a) ease of introducing experimental variation (b) administrative permission etc. considerably influenced selection of experimental and control group, and these institution came out to be, the Faculty of Education, SSJ Campus, Almora as the control group and Presentation College of Teacher Education, Kathgodam as the experimental group.

3.2.2 Sampling Method

For experimental purpose, a group of thirty-five (35) subjects from each of two selected institutions were randomly assigned to experimental and control groups. Statistical equivalence between control and experimental groups was statistically tested on selected independent and dependent variables at pretest stage. Here, experimental group was provided assertiveness training through a specifically designed training programme as adapted from Bishop (1996), whereas no such treatment was introduced in the control group.

3.2.3 Testing Equivalence between Experimental and Control groups on Socio-demographic Factors and Dependent Variables at Pretest Stage

In order to establish statistical equivalence between control and experimental groups, Chi-square test was employed to compare frequencies on selected independent variables viz. caste-group, income group, fathers' occupational group, fathers' educational status and academic achievement of the trainees, whereas, t-test was used to compare mean differences between the two groups of teacher trainees on level of assertiveness, self acceptance and academic achievement motivation. Table 3.20, and related data presented in Figure- 3.12 present the number and percentages of trainees in the control and experimental groups belonging to different caste groups.

Table 3.20: Caste-group wise Composition of Control and Experimental groups*

Caste	Number of Trainees in Institution		Total	Chi-Square value	Degree of freedom	Sig. at 0.05 level
	Control Group	Experimental Group				
Gen	24 (68.6)	26 (74.3)	50(71.4)	1.70	3	Not – Sig.
OBC	5 (14.3)	2 (5.7)	7 (10.0)			
SC	5 (14.3)	5 (14.3)	10 (14.3)			
ST	1 (2.9)	2 (5.7)	3 (4.3)			
Total	35 (100)	35(100)	70 (100)			

*Figures in parentheses are percentage

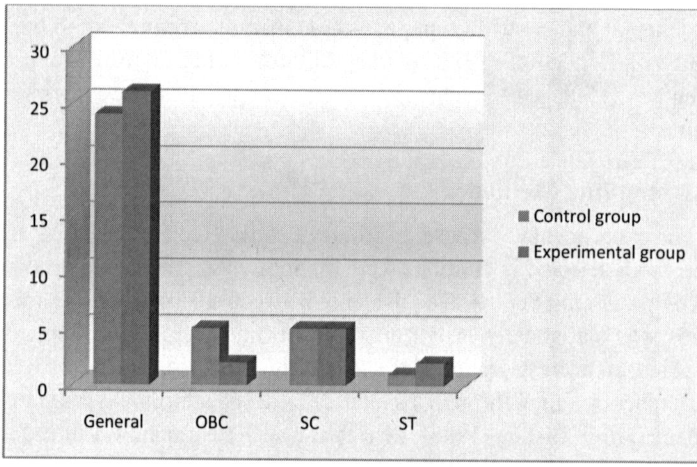

Figure 3.12: Caste-group wise Composition of Control and Experimental groups

It may be observed from Table 3.20, that majority of the respondents belonged to General Caste category, i.e. 68.6% and 74.3%, in both control and experimental groups. The Other Backward Castes Category was represented by 14.3% in control group and 5.7% in the experimental group. Percentages of respondents belonging to Scheduled Castes groups (14.3) were observed to be similar in the two groups. Scheduled Tribes were represented by 2.9% and about 6 percent respondents (See also, Fig. 3.12). The Chi-square value obtained for this distribution revealed that caste wise composition of experimental and control groups was more or less similar and did not differ at 0.05 level of significance.

Table 3.21, and related data presented in Figure 3.13, show number and percentages of trainees in the control and experimental groups belonging to families with different monthly income groups.

Table 3.21: Composition of Control and Experimental groups in terms of Monthly Income of their Families

Monthly income group	Number of Trainees		Total	Chi-Square value	Degree of freedom	Sig. at 0.05 level
	Control Group	Experimental Group				
Low income group	13 (37.1)	9 (25.7)	22 (31.4)	1.11	2	Not – Sig.
Average income group	12 (34.3)	15 (42.9)	27 (38.6)			
High income group	10 (28.6)	11 (31.4)	21 (30.0)			
Total	35 (100)	35 (100)	70 (100)			

* Figures in parentheses are percentages.

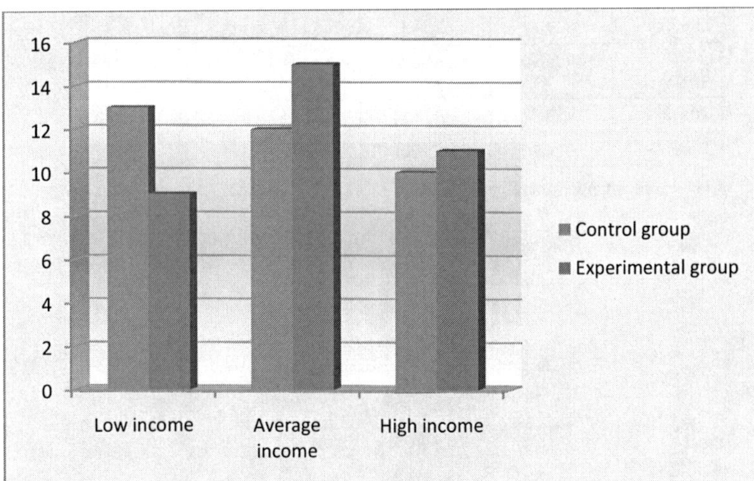

Figure 3.13: Family-income wise Composition of Control and Experimental groups

With respect to monthly income of families, it may be observed from Table 3.21, and Figure 3.13, that number and percentages of trainees belonging to low income group was respectively 37.1% and 25.7% in control and experimental groups. Number of respondents corresponding to average income category was observed to be 34.3% in control group and 42.9% in the experimental group. The high income category was represented by 28.6% respondents in control group and 31.4% in the experimental group. Table 3.21 suggests that the maximum percentage of trainees in the control group belonged to low income category, whereas in the experimental group it was the average income category which had the majority of respondents.

However, Chi-square value, obtained for the distribution of teacher-trainees in experimental and control groups, was non-significant at 0.05 level of significance, showing the two groups to be more or less similar.

Composition of control and experimental groups on the basis of father's occupation are shown in Table 3.22 and in Figure 3.14.

Table 3.22: Father's Occupation-wise Composition of Control and Experimental groups*

Father's occupation group	Number of Trainees		Total	Chi-Square value	Degree of freedom	Sig. at 0.05 level
	Control Group	Experimental Group				
Farming	6(17.1)	3(8.6)	9(12.9)	3.33	3	Not - Sig.
Teaching	4(11.4)	2(5.7)	6(8.6)			
Govt. employee	20(57.1)	20(57.1)	40(57.1)			
Others	5(14.3)	10(28.6)	15(21.4)			
Total	35(100)	35(100)	70(100)			

* Figures in parentheses are percentages

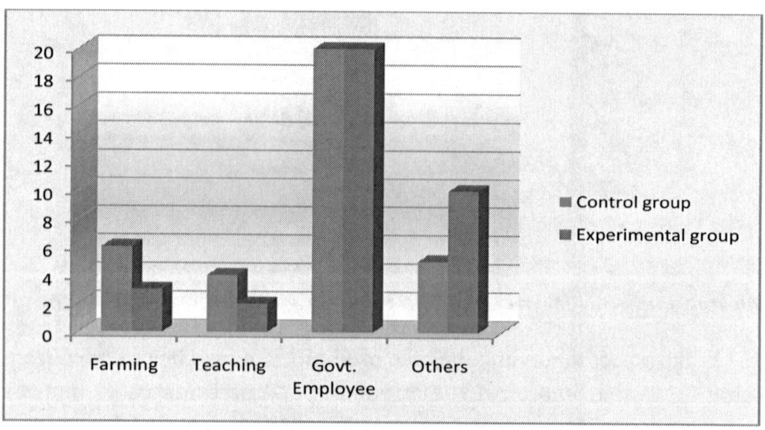

Figure 3.14: Father's Occupation-wise Composition of Control and Experimental groups

Table 3.22 presents father's occupation wise composition of control and experimental groups. A majority of respondents (57.1%) were found to be belonging to fathers working as 'government employees' in both the groups, whereas the number and percentages of trainees in control and experimental groups belonging to fathers carrying out 'other' occupations were 14.3% and 28.6% respectively (Fig.3.14). Respondents who belonged to fathers in 'farming' occupation were found to be 17.1% in control group and 8.6 % in the experimental group. 'Teaching' as father's occupation was represented by 11.4% trainees in control group and around 6% in the experimental group. However, father's occupation wise composition of experimental and control groups was found to be more or less similar, as the Chi-square value obtained for the distribution did not differ at 0.05 level of significance.

Composition of control and experimental groups on the basis of father's education are shown in Table 3.23 and in Figure 3.15.

Table 3.23: Composition of Control and Experimental groups on the basis of Father's Education*

Father's education group	Number of Trainees		Total	Chi-Square value	Degree of freedom	Sig. at 0.05 level
	Control Group	Experimental Group				
Illiterate	1(2.9)	2(5.7)	3(4.3)	4.59	4	Not - Sig.
Primary	4(11.4)	1(2.9)	5(7.1)			
Secondary	16(45.7)	16(45.7)	32(45.7)			
Graduation	10(28.6)	7(20.0)	17(24.3)			
Post-graduate & above	4(11.4)	9(25.7)	13(18.6)			
Total	35(100)	35(100)	70(100)			

*Figures in parentheses are percentages

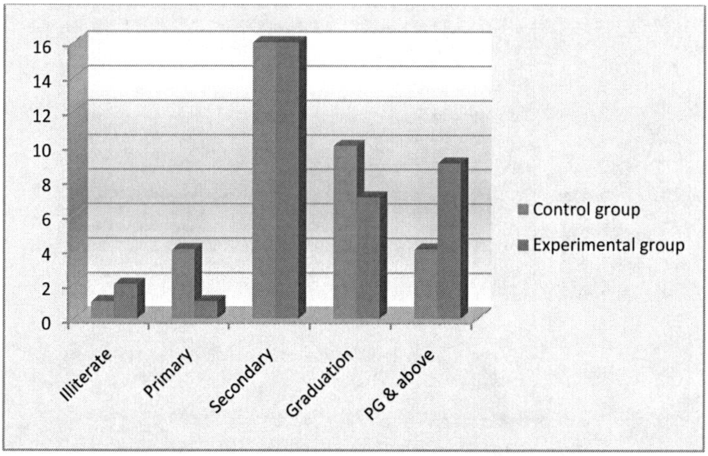

Figure 3.15: Father's Education wise Composition of Control and Experimental groups

Father's education wise composition of control and experimental groups were compared in Table 3.23, where it may be observed that maximum percentages of trainees, i.e. 45.7%, in both the control and experimental groups belonged to fathers with 'secondary' level of educational status. About 3% respondents belonging to 'illiterate' fathers were found in control group, whereas similar percent of the trainees belonging to fathers with 'primary' level of education was represented in experimental group. Percentages of respondents belonging to 'graduate' fathers were observed to be more or less similar in the two groups i.e. 28.6% in the control and 20% in the experimental group. Fathers educated to 'post-graduation' level

Table 3.24: Composition of Control and Experimental groups on the basis of Mother's Education*

Mother's education group	Number of Trainees		Total	Chi-Square value	Degree of freedom	Sig. at 0.05 level
	Control Group	Experimental Group				
Illiterate	1(2.9)	7(20.0)	8(11.4)	9.83	4	Sig.
Primary	17(48.6)	7(20.0)	24(34.3)			
Secondary	12(34.3)	12(34.3)	24(34.3)			
Graduation	3(8.6)	5(14.3)	8(11.4)			
Post-graduate & above	2(5.7)	4(11.4)	6(8.6)			
Total	35(100)	35(100)	70(100)			

* Figures in parentheses are percentages.

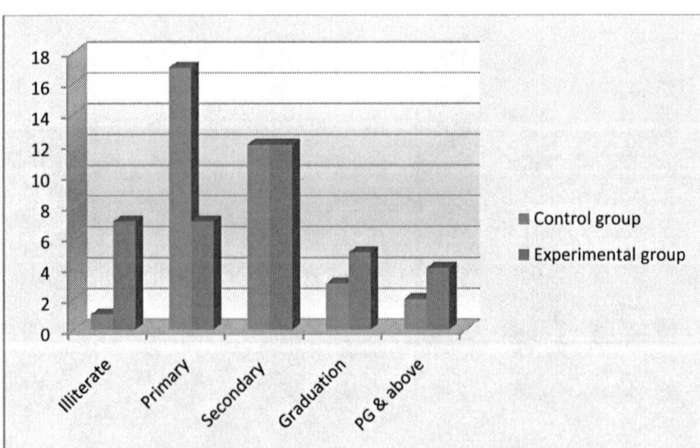

Figure 3.16: Mother's Education wise Compositionof Control and Experimental groups

and above were represented by 11.4% and about 26 % respondents respectively in control and experimental groups. The Chi-square value obtained for the distribution did not reveal any significant difference in the father's education wise composition of experimental and control groups at 0.05 level of significance. Composition of control and experimental groups on the basis of mother's education is shown in Table 3.24 and in Figure 3.16.

It may be observed from Table 3.24 that maximum percentage of trainees i.e. 48.6% in the control group belonged to mothers educated up to 'primary' level, whereas maximum percentage of trainees in the experimental group (34.3%) belonged to mothers educated up to 'secondary' level. A minimum of about 3% respondents belonging to 'illiterate' mothers was found in the control group. On the other hand, minimum percentage of trainees in experimental group was found to belong to 'post graduate' mothers. In experimental group, a similar percent (20.0) of trainees reported to be belonging 'illiterate' mothers and mothers with primary level of education. Mothers educated to graduation level were represented by 8.6 and about 14 percent respondents respectively in control and experimental groups. Mother's education wise composition of experimental and control groups were revealed to be significantly different as the Chi- square value obtained for the distribution was found to be significant at 0.05 level.

Table 3.25 and related data presented in Figure 3.17 show the number and percentages of trainees in control and experimental groups belonging to different academic achievement status.

Table 3.25: Academic Achievement wise Composition of Control and Experimental groups*

Academic achievement group	Number of Trainees		Total	Chi-Square value	Degree of freedom	Sig. at 0.05 level
	Control Group	Experimental Group				
Low academic achievement	08 (22.9)	09 (25.7)	17 (24.3)	2.62	2	Not-Sig.
Average academic achievement	14 (40.0)	19 (54.3)	33(47.1)			
High academic achievement	13 (37.1)	07 (20.0)	20 (28.6)			
Total	35(100)	35(100)	70(100)			

* Figures in parentheses are percentages.

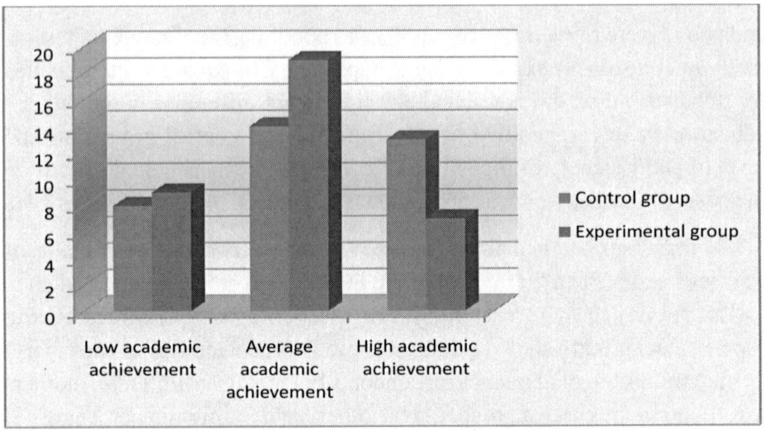

Figure 3.17: Academic Achievement wise Composition of Control and Experimental groups

It is evident from Table 3.25 and Figure 3.17 that maximum percentages of trainees in both the control and experimental groups had an average academic achievement status, represented by 40% and about 54% trainees respectively in the two groups. About 23% respondents having low academic achievement were found in control group, whereas 25.7 percent of the trainees of low academic achievement category were represented in experimental group. Percentages of respondents with high academic achievement were observed to be about 37% in the control and 20% in the experimental group. Here also, the distribution did not reveal statistically significant difference in academic achievement wise composition of experimental and control groups (at 0.05 level).

In order to compare mean difference between the two groups of teacher trainees on level of assertiveness, self acceptance and academic achievement motivation, t-test was used and following Tables present analysis carried out in this manner. Table 3.26 and Figure- 3.18 show the mean scores obtained by respondents of control and experimental groups on level of assertiveness.

Table 3.26: Comparison of Female Teacher-trainees from Control and Experimental groups on Level of Assertiveness at Pretest Stage

Group	Number	Mean	Standard Deviation	t-value	Significance at 0.05 level
Control	35	212.57	19.91	0.25	Not – Significant
Experimental	35	211.37	19.71		

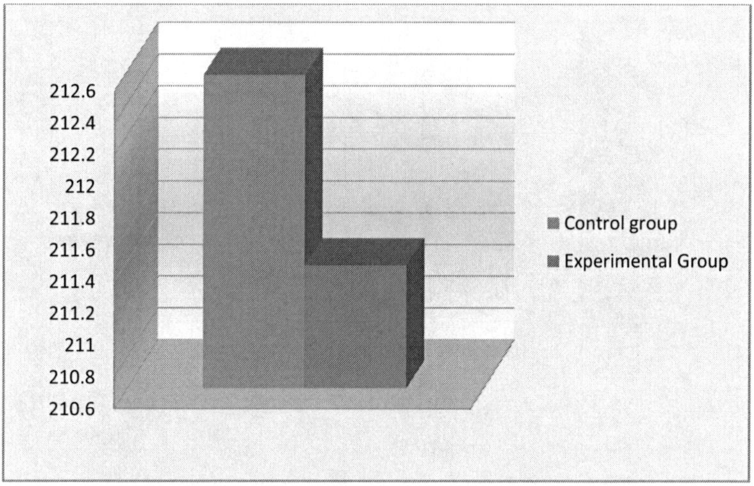

Figure 3.18: Mean scores on Assertiveness obtained Respondents of Control and Experimental groups at Pretest Stage

An observation of Table 3.26 and Figure 3.18 revealed that mean of assertiveness scores obtained by teacher-trainees of control group (m=212.57) was slightly higher than the mean score (211.37) obtained by trainees of experimental group. This may probably because trainees in the control group, i.e. from the campus of the university, found more opportunities for expression of self in the form of co-curricular activities in comparison to the trainees from the self-financed institution which was selected for intervention. However, t-value (0.25) was not found to be significant at 0.05 level of significance, which means that the two groups did not differ in level of assertiveness significantly.

Table 3.27 and Figure 3.19 show mean scores obtained by respondents of control and experimental groups on level of self-acceptance whereas Table 3.28 and Figure 3.20 presents data related to analysis of mean scores on academic achievement motivation level of teacher-trainees in the two groups.

Table 3.27: Comparison of Female Teacher-trainees from Control and Experimental groups on Level of Self-acceptance at Pretest Stage

Group	Number	Mean	Standard Deviation	t-value	Significance at 0.05 level
Control	35	15.77	2.34	1.35	Not-Significant
Experimental	35	16.77	3.69		

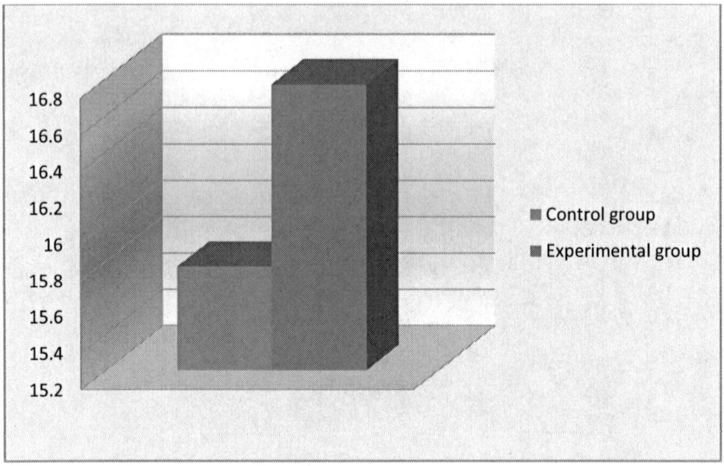

Figure 3.19: Mean scores on Self-acceptance obtained by Respondents of Control and Experimental groups at Pretest Stage

Table 3.28: Comparison of Female Teacher-trainees of Control and Experimental groups on Level of Academic Achievement Motivation at Pretest Stage

Group	Number	Mean	Standard Deviation	t-value	Significance at 0.05 level
Control	35	30.46	3.33	1.20	Not – Significant
Experimental	35	29.57	2.82		

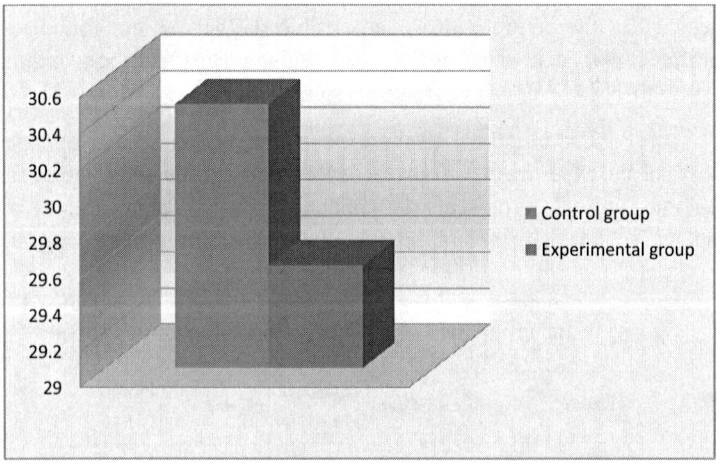

Figure 3.20: Mean scores on Academic Achievement Motivation obtained by Respondents of Control and Experimental groups at Pretest Stage

It is indicated in Table 3.27 and Table 3.28 that trainees of control group did not differ from trainees selected in experimental group on level of self-acceptance and level of academic achievement motivation as the respective t-values were not found to be significant at 0.05 level. Reason behind this pattern may be the observed similarities among teacher-trainees selected in the two groups on different socio-demographic and personal characteristics. Thus, individuals selected in control and experimental groups did not differ in their level of self-acceptance and academic achievement motivation.

It may be concluded from analysis carried out in section-3.2.3 that the two groups selected for control and experimental treatment were similar on caste group membership, family income, father's occupation, father's education and academic achievement of female teacher-trainees.No significant difference was also observed between the two groups on selected dependent variables of assertiveness, self-acceptance and academic achievement motivation at pretest stage. However, significant difference was observed in mother's education wise composition of two groups. This particular limitation was beyond the control of researcher and may be taken to as a limitation of the experimental design in social and institutional settings. As it was stated earlier, that facilities and ease of introducing experimental variation, administrative permission etc. were expected to considerably influence selection of experimental and control groups, the two groups of teacher-trainees from Faculty of Education, SSJ Campus, Almora and Presentation College of Teacher Education, Kathgodam were finally selected for assigning control and experimental treatment respectively.

3.2.4 Assertiveness Training Programme

An assertiveness training programme designed to improve individual's assertive beliefs and behaviours, adapted by Dhoundiyal (2005) in congruence with assertiveness skill training developed by Sue Bishop (1996) and including components of Self awareness, Awareness of rights , Refining goals, Nurturing self esteem , Feeling talk, Awareness of reasons of non-assertion, Ability to handle putdowns, Awareness of one's body language, Developing assertive body language, Being able to say ' No', Being able to make requests , Skill of handling conflicts, Ability to identify stereotypes, Handling discrepant situations etc., was used as main intervention in the experimental design.

Although, it was proposed that assertiveness training will be provided to female teacher-trainees of one randomly selected B.Ed. training institution for a duration of about two hours per day, extended over 30 working days during an academic session, but due to certain limitations of time, completion of curriculum and administrative permission etc. the investigator decided to conduct this programme of assertiveness training in the form day long workshop, extended over six working days, divided into twelve technical sessions, among 35 subjects in a specified hall at the selected institution. Training programme included tasks of short presentations, group discussion, role playing, group-play, feedback from peers and from the coordinator in the form of exercises on above stated components (see Appendix-5).

3.2.5 Overview of Assertiveness Training Sessions (Experimental Treatment)

Day I

The first day of training workshop started with opening statements made by Dean, Faculty of Education, K U Nainital, Prof. N.C. Dhoundiyal, himself who have undertaken adaptation of this training programme in Indian conditions. The introduction session was followed by setting of Ground rules and a Contract, defining the general code of conduct, which was signed by the trainees.

In first technical session, Prof. Dhoundiyal profoundly oriented trainees on the topic 'Our Behaviour & Personality', after which trainees were asked to list the characteristics of behaviour pattern expressed by different individuals in their close contacts (Individual Exercise-1). The second presentation in session was made by investigator for developing an 'Understanding of Personality', which was followed by completing Individual Exercise-2: 'Test of the concept of personality'. In this exercise trainees were required to check statements which they felt to be true in the context of personality. These were later discussed in main group. Second session after lunch break, began with short introduction on 'Interpersonal behaviour & Personality' by investigator, after which trainees were asked to classify the behaviour patterns listed in Individual Exercise-3, into four different personality types. The related discussion on this exercise was held again in main group. Thus, first day activities were closed after thanking all the participants.

Day II

The third session on second day started with welcome statements and presentation of reports of previous day's work by nominated participants. The investigator, after a short introduction of topic initiated group discussion on 'Personality Patterns', and allotted Group Exercises- 4.1 and 4.2. Where in exercise-4.1, participants were required to enlist characteristics of persons with four different personality types in social and interpersonal situations, and in exercise-4.2, they were asked to report commonly observed behaviour exhibited by four personality types in suggested social and interpersonal situations. Presentation of group reports by participants on exercises- 4.1.and 4.2 and related discussion/ summarization were followed in consolidated main group. After a short tea break, investigator initiated talk on 'Relationship between personality & Life', and assigned Individual Exercise-5, to the participnts in which trainees were asked to indicate the felt level of success by persons with four different personality types in suggested areas of life. The related discussion was conducted in main consolidated group.

The fourth (post-lunch) session highlighted presentation on 'Which Personality Pattern you want for yourself?' and related Exercise-6, which was in the form of a declaration made by trainees to adopt a particular type of personality pattern, which turned out to be assertive behaviour. Next presentation on 'Assertive Personality: Identify your Needs and be Selfaware', was made by investigator and broadly discussed the characteristics of assertive personality, with stress on identification of needs of an individual in different social and interpersonal situations. The second day activities were closed by assigning an Exercise -7 to be done at home by the participants.

Day III

Fifth technical session on third day of training workshop began with usual welcome statements and presentation of report of previous day's work. The researcher, after a short introduction of the topic 'Characteristics of Assertiveness in Personality' initiated individual reading, followed by group exercise, on discussion of personality patterns adopted by trainees in personal and social situations which were summarized in main group. In next presentation titled, 'My own Assertiveness Development Programme', investigator encouraged participants to examine the personality pattern adopted by them at present in various situations in the form of Exercise-8 A, followed by small group discussion and main group consolidation. This leads to subsequent development of assertiveness programme by participants for themselves in Exercise-8 B. Individual Exercise-10, then assigned to the participants which required them to complete some statements related to their qualities, abilities, achievements, followed by the presentation of 'Self' in main group with full confidence.

Post-lunch session VI th entailed presentations on 'Refining your Goals' and 'Feeling Talk' followed by home assignment (Exercise-9), which was related to identifications of personal needs, defining objectives in short and long run with subsequent management of time of attaining these objectives by participants.

Day IV

Fourth day of training programme started with VII th technical session, which was marked by welcome statements and presentation of previous day's report. Initially, researcher continued a short discussion on previous day's topic of 'Feeling talk', which was followed through role plays carried out by participants (in groups of three) in different situations suggested in Exercise-11. Experiences related to the exercise were shared and discussed in main group. The investigator, in next presentation, introduced topic, 'When we don't assert? Why?' which was followed by group activity of completing statements related to identification of situations in which participants find ease or difficulty in adopting assertive behaviour (Exercise-12), followed by main group discussion.

Post-lunch session VIII th highlighted presentation on 'Handling Put downs', followed by sub-group exercises- 13-A and B, related to identification of different statements of putdowns and classification of different patterns of behaviour adopted in response to these putdowns into four main personality types. Responses on these exercises were discussed in main group. Exercise 13-C afterwards, provided participants a chance to perform role plays in handling one common put down in everyday situations. The day activities were closed after initiating discussion on 'Body Language' and home assignment of reading Exercise-14A, related to the identification of different components of body language.

Day V

Ninth session on fifth day embarked with usual welcome and presentation of report on previous day's work. The investigator initiated sub-group Exercises 14-A and 14-B, after a short review of topic 'Body Language'. These exercises were mainly related to identification of different components of body language and their association with four main personality patterns in a group situation. Completion of exercises by participants was followed by discussion in main group. The next activity entailed presentation on 'Using Body Language Assertively' and a related Exercise 14-C. It provided chance to participants for role playing in group situation using assertive body language, followed by discussion in main group. The post-lunch session X th comprised of presentation on 'Making a Request', followed by Exercise-16, in which participants were required to identify and enlist the factors to be consider while a request is made and to examine the characteristics of request made by persons with four different personality types. Day activities were closed after role playing by participants in making request assertively followed by main group discussion.

Day VI

Pre-lunch session XI th on sixth and final day of training workshop started with routine welcome and presentation of previous day's report. A presentation on 'Handling Conflict' by investigator highlighted the concept at the beginning. It was followed by Exercises-17 and 18, which required participants to generate an understanding of different behaviour patterns adopted by individuals in handing conflicts by means of individual reading and group discussion. This also stressed on derivation of most appropriate way to overcome such situations by participants. The process was followed by discussion in main group. The next presentation of session, after a short tea break, was related to the concept of 'Stereotypes'. In related Exercise-19, participants were asked to list some common behavioural characteristics associated with men and women. These were later discussed in main group. Post-lunch session XIIth entailed presentation on topic 'Barriers due to Stereotypes', which was followed by Exercises-20 A & 20 B. These exercises required participants to identify barriers in social situations commonly faced by them as women, which limits their progress as an individual. The problems identified through sub-group discussion were then discussed in main group.

In process of closing the six days assertiveness training workshop, a posttest was assigned to participants, which they returned after completion in a specified time. In the closing session, comments were invited from participants about the programme, which were found to be highly satisfactory. The Principal as well as the Academic- Director of the institution inspired and motivated participants to imbibe benefits of programme by adopting modification of their personality in an appropriate manner. The investigator closed the workshop with thanking all the participants and conveying a special thank to administration and staff of the institution.

3.2.6 Research Tools for Data Collection

The following research tools, used at survey stage were employed again for the purpose of data collection at experimental stage:

- Assertive Behaviour Assessment Scale (ABAS)
- Self-Acceptance Inventory (KSAI-K) developed by Kakkar (2010).
- Academic Achievement Motivation Test (AAMT) developed by Sharma (2010).

  The detailed description of these tools has already been given at survey stage.

3.2.7 Data Collection Procedure at Experimental Stage

The data collection procedure at experimental stage comprised of

Posttest, which consisted of two stages:

- **Data Collection in Experimental Group**, and
- **Data Collection in Control Group**

Data Collection in Experimental Group: To study the effect of training in assertiveness on study variables, viz. assertiveness, self-acceptance and academic achievement motivation among female teacher-trainees, posttest was organized in same group of thirty–five subjects who were given assertiveness training. The four research tools were reused in the similar manner in posttest as in stage I. Posttest was carried out immediately after completion of assertiveness training in the experimental group.

Data Collection in Control Group: The investigator with the permission of Head, collected data from those thirty-five female teacher-trainees from control group whom data were collected at pretest stage. Female trainees were asked to fill four questionnaires again at this stage after proper explanation of nature and purpose of testing. General instructions were also adequately provided to them so as to avoid consultation with their fellow trainees.

Thus, similar to survey stage, data from experimental and control group were collected in a supervised testing and group situation.

3.2.8 Method of Data Analysis at Experimental Stage

In the light of aims and objectives of study, data obtained at posttest stage were analyzed by making use of inferential statistical methods. A Chi-square test was employed to establish statistical equivalence between control and experimental group at pretest stage. Here, t-test was used to compare mean difference among control and experimental groups of female teacher-trainees on selected dependent variables. One-way analysis of variance was also carried out to find interaction between selected independent variables on measure of assertiveness within experimental group. Results obtained through data analysis of experimental stage are presented and discussed in chapter on data analysis and interpretation.

Chapter - 4

Data Analysis and Interpretation

4.0.0 Data Analysis and Interpretation

As par to the aims and objectives of present research, data obtained for the present study were analyzed along following dimensions:

4.1. Comparison of level of assertiveness in population subgroups classified on the basis of following characteristics:

1. Caste group
2. Income group
3. Father's occupational group
4. Parents educational status
5. Academic achievement group

4.2. Comparison of effect of specifically designed assertiveness training programme on following characteristics of female teacher- trainees between control and experimental subgroups.

1. Level of assertiveness
2. Level of self acceptance
3. Level of academic achievement motivation

4.3. Comparison of effect of assertiveness training programme on level of assertiveness in groups of female teacher-trainees identified on the basis of :

vi Caste

vii Family income

viii Occupational background of family

ix Parent's educational status and

x Academic achievement

The above mentioned aspects of data analysis were associated with the following objectives of the study:

1. Identification of personal, social and academic characteristics that interact with assertiveness of female teacher-trainees.
2. Identification of effect of assertiveness training programme on assertiveness among female teacher-trainees in control and experimental subgroups.
3. Identification of effect of assertiveness training programme on self-acceptance among female teacher-trainees in control and experimental subgroups.
4. Identification of effect of assertiveness training programme on academic achievement motivation among female teachertrainees in control and experimental subgroups.
5. Identification of effect of assertiveness training programme on level of assertiveness in groups of female teacher-trainees identified on the basis of personal and socio-demographic characteristics.

Various hypotheses proposed to be tested through this study were organized along above mentioned objectives. Test of these hypotheses was undertaken through employing analysis of variance, taking independent and dependent variables in accordance to the requirement of particular hypotheses. Data analysis carried out in view of above considerations is elaborated in following sections.

4.1.0 Comparison of Level of Assertiveness among various Subgroups of Female Teacher-trainees

Table 4.1.0 shows the distribution of level of assertiveness found among female teacher trainees selected in the sample.

It may be observed from Table 4.1.0 that assertiveness scores obtained by female teacher-trainees ranged from a minimum of 115.00 to a maximum of 270.00. Mean value of this distribution was 203.37, with a standard deviation of 24.08. The values of mean, median and mode of this distribution were found to be more or less equal. Hence, it can be said that assertiveness scores obtained by the respondents tended to be more or less normal, though skewness value (-0.28) of distribution indicated it to be slightly negatively skewed, with a peakedness value of 0.47 . Twenty five percent of the trainees obtained a score of 189 and below, while the uppermost quartile was represented by trainees obtaining a score of 220.00 and above.

Table 4.1.0: Distribution of Level of Assertiveness among Female Teacher-trainees

Assertiveness score (class-interval)	Frequency	Percent frequency	Statistical indices
265-274	02	0.6	Mean= 203.37
255-264	03	0.8	Median= 204.00
245-254	12	3.1	Mode= 203.00
235-244	16	4.2	SD = 24.08
225-234	41	10.4	Skewness = -0.28
215-224	53	13.5	Kurtosis = 0.47
205-214	64	16.3	Q1= 189.00
195-204	70	17.7	Q3= 220.25
185-194	56	14.2	Minimum value=115
175-184	32	8.1	Maximum value= 270
165-174	24	6.2	
155-164	08	2.1	
145-154	07	1.9	
135-144	03	0.9	
125-134	02	0.6	
115-124	01	0.3	
Total	394	100	

4.1.1 Caste group of Teacher-trainees and Level of Assertiveness

Four caste groups were represented in the sample of present study. These were General Castes, Other Backward Castes, Schedule Castes and Schedule Tribes. Majority of the respondents belonged to General Caste category (68.5%), while Other Backward Categories, Scheduled Castes and Scheduled Tribes were represented by 13.2, 13.5 and about 4.8 percent respondents respectively. As the role of caste has considerable influence in shaping socio-cultural experiences in Indian society, it was considered significant to analyze the interaction of caste-group membership with level of assertiveness among female teacher trainees.

Table 4.2.0 presents the mean and standard deviation values of assertiveness scores of female trainees of different caste groups, while Table 4.2.1 presents results obtained through analysis of variance with caste group membership as independent variable and scores on assertiveness as dependent variable. The means on assertiveness for different caste groups of respondents have also been shown in Fig. 4.1

Table 4.2.0: Comparison of Level of Assertiveness among Teacher trainees belonging to different Caste groups

Caste groups	Number	Mean	Standard Deviation
General	270	203.95	24.46
OBC	52	202.38	20.27
SC	53	202.00	22.94
ST	19	201.68	31.89

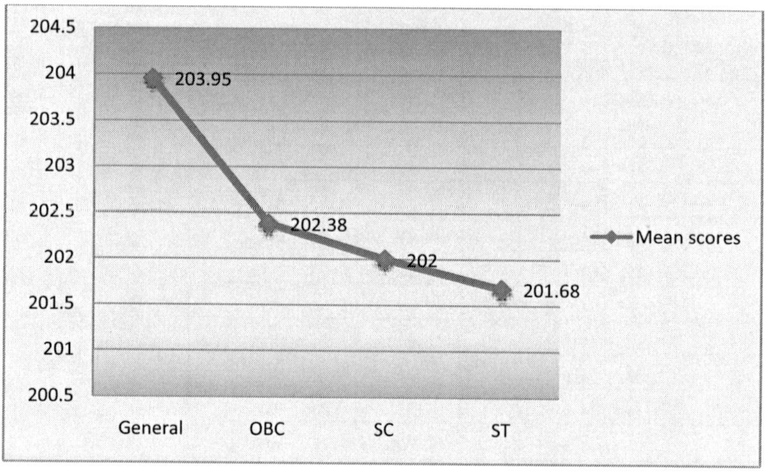

Figure 4.1: Mean scores obtained by Respondents of different Caste groups

It may be observed from Table 4.2.0 and Fig-4.1 that the mean value on assertiveness associated with trainees belonging to Other Backward Caste group was 202.38. The mean value on assertive behaviour shown by trainees belonging to Scheduled Caste group (202.00) was more or less similar to the mean of Other Backward Caste group of trainees. Scheduled Tribe trainees scored a mean value of 201.68, which is slightly lower than the mean value obtained by trainees of Other Backward Caste and Scheduled Caste groups. The highest mean was found to be associated with trainees of General Caste group (m=203.95), indicating that in the sample studied in the present study, it were the General Caste trainees, who showed a highest level of assertiveness in behaviour. However, when the data were subjected to analysis of variance (Table 4.2.1), the differences between groups came out to be statistically non-significant at 0.05 level of significance.

Table 4.2.1: Results of ANOVA of Assertiveness scores of Teacher trainees belonging to different Caste groups

Source of variation	Sum of squares	Degree of freedom	Mean square	F-value	Significance at 0.05 level
Between groups	294.21	3	98.07	0.17	Not-significant
Within groups	227647.69	390	583.71		
Total	227941.90	393			

This particular finding revealed that the caste group membership does not play a significant role in shaping level of assertiveness among teacher-trainees. In this context, findings obtained by Sue, et. al. (1990) are pertinent, which revealed that Chinese-American women were as assertive as Caucasian subjects on all behavioural measures. Working in Indian socio-cultural context, Gangwar (2012) also found that caste group membership do not influence level of assertive behaviour among secondary school students. Contrary to this trend of findings, Rodriquez (2001) revealed a significant interaction between ethnicity and assertiveness among Hispanic college women. Lineberger and Calhoun (1983) and Bell and Jackson (1984), on the other hand, focused on Black and White undergraduates and found significant difference in their level of assertiveness. Higher level of assertiveness was also noticed among Black preschool students by Weigel (2006). In this connection Yoshioka (2000) has suggested that assertiveness may have culturally relative definitions associated with the values upheld by different societies.

4.1.1 Income group and Level of Assertiveness

Parental behaviour and general environment within home may be expected to get shaped considerably by income of parents or family to which a trainee belongs. Families varying in this context are likely to affect behavioural patterns among their female wards, and thus may develop have different levels of assertiveness in behaviour. Data of present study were analyzed to explore this aspect. Table 4.3.0 and Table 4.3.1 present results of this analysis (see also Fig.4.2).

Table 4.3.0: Comparison of Level of Assertiveness among Teachertrainees belonging to Families with different Monthly Income

Income group	Number	Mean	Standard Deviation
Low income group (Rs. 8875 & below)	98	202.16	25.64
Average income group (Rs. 8876 to 24999)	190	202.94	23.73
High income group (Rs.25000 & above)	106	205.26	23.34

As reported earlier, teacher-trainees in present study belonged to families earning a monthly income from a minimum of Rs.700 to Rs.80, 000. The mean income level was found to be Rs.17,428/month. This distribution of income level was subdivided into three income levels on the basis of Q1 (Rs.8, 875) and Q3 (Rs.25, 000) values. Ninety-eight trainees were found to be belonging to low income group (Rs. 8875 & below), while 106 trainees belonged to high income group (Rs.25000 & above). Majority of 190 trainees belonged to average income group.

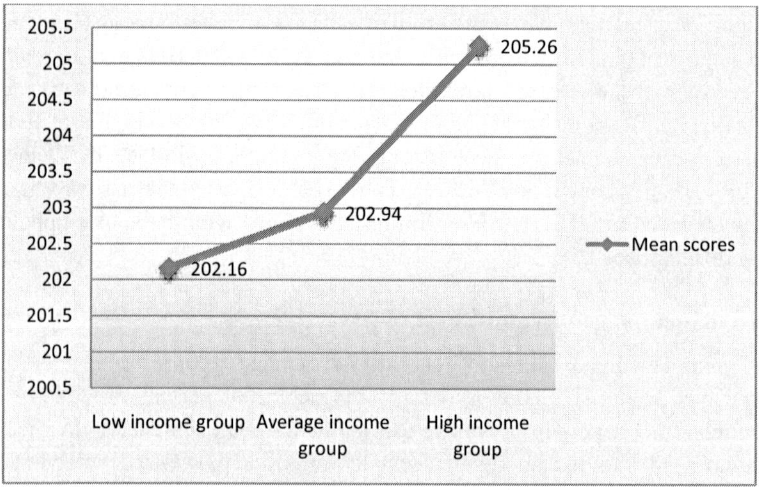

Figure 4.2: Mean scores obtained by Respondents belonging to Families of different Income groups

Table 4.3.1: Results of ANOVA of Assertiveness scores of Teacher trainees belonging to Families of three Income levels

Source of variance	Sum of squares	Degree of freedom	Mean square	F-value	Significance at 0.05 level
Between groups	558.66	2	279.33	0.48	Not-Significant
Within groups	227383.23	391	581.54		
Total	227941.90	393			

An observation of Table 4.3.0 reveals that mean value on assertiveness scores attained a higher level in the group which was higher on income (Fig.4.2). However, results obtained through analysis of variance yielded a non-significant F-value at 0.05 level of significance. Here, findings revealed that income level of the family does not have a significant influence on level of assertiveness among teacher-trainees. A number of studies have attempted to analyze the influence of family income on individual's level of assertiveness. In congruence to the findings of present study, Gangwar (2012) has also revealed that income level of family does not have an influence on assertive behaviour of their wards.

However, certain researches have obtained different results on the same variables. For example, Ibrahim (2011) revealed that there is a positive relationship between family income and student's level of assertiveness and psychological empowerment. In this connection, a positive correlation between socio-economic status and the level of assertiveness among Greek students was also obtained by Patera and Politynou (2008). Findings obtained by Mueen et. al. (2006) and Mentes (2007) have also revealed significant interaction between socio-economic status and level of assertiveness of students.

4.1.3. Father's Occupation and Trainee's Level of Assertiveness

Analysis of father's occupation as a factor in shaping assertiveness among female teacher trainees has the implicit assumption that primary occupation carried out by father not only interacts with income level but also has a considerable influence on the general environment of home. Different categories of occupational groups and different types of home environments created thereof are, thus, expected to have a potential in influencing development and expression of assertiveness among their wards, particularly the female wards, of the family. Comparison of level of assertiveness among teacher-trainees belonging to fathers with different occupational groups is presented in Table 4.4.0, and Table 4.4.1 present results of analysis of variance carried out in this context. The mean values on assertiveness of female teacher-trainees belonging to fathers with different occupational groups are also shown in Figure 4.3.

Table 4.4.0: Comparison of Assertiveness among Teacher-trainees belonging to Fathers with different Occupational groups

Occupational groups	Number	Mean	Standard Deviation
Farming	53	205.13	26.97
Teaching	44	210.34	23.55
Government Employee	224	201.87	22.97
Others	73	202.49	25.20

Table 4.4.1: Results of ANOVA of Assertiveness scores of Teacher – trainees belonging to Fathers with different Occupational groups

Source of variance	Sum of squares	Degree of freedom	Mean square	F -value	Significance at 0.05 level
Between groups	2862.44	3	954.15	1.65	Not-Significant
Within groups	225079.45	390	577.13		
Total	227941.90	393			

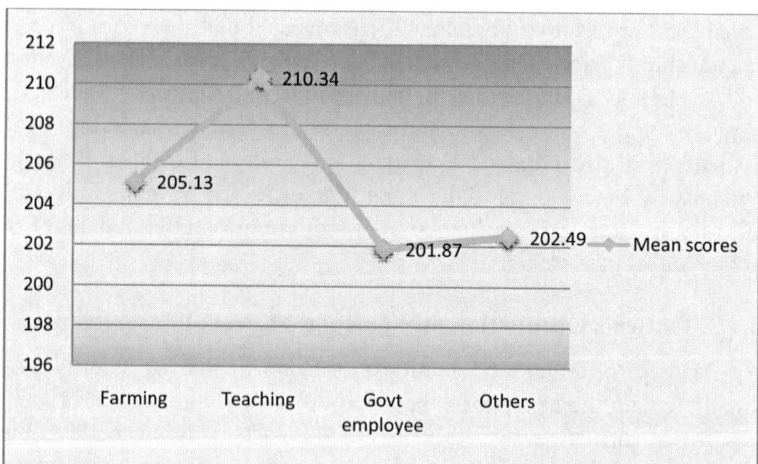

Figure 4.3: Mean scores obtained by Respondents belonging to Fathers engaged in different Occupations

It may be observed from Table 4.4.0 that the highest mean on assertiveness score (m=210.34) was associated with trainees whose father carried out 'teaching' as their primary occupation. The next higher level of mean on assertiveness (m=205.13) was associated with trainees whose fathers were in 'farming' occupation. Mean assertiveness of trainees belonging to 'government employee' and 'others' were more or less equal, being represented by respective means of 201.87 and 202.49 only. Trainees belonging to 'government employee' and 'others' occupational groups appear to be lower in assertiveness as compared to the other two occupational groups.

Results of analysis of variance shown in Table 4.4.1, however, did not indicate presence of statistically significant differences among the groups. This result was congruent with results of Ibrahim (2015), who revealed non-significant relationship between occupation carried out by parents and assertiveness level of high school students. This finding was however contrary to the findings obtained by Mentes (2007) and Gangwar (2012), who found significant interaction between father's occupation and level of assertiveness among high school students. It may be stated that occupation carried out by father does interact with income level and has influence on the general environment of home but the potential in influencing development and expression of assertiveness among their wards decreases after certain age and educational levels. Respondents of present study are more mature as compared to secondary level students and they may be expected to be having a better understanding of their socio-cultural contexts; thus, relying more on their own abilities, having better sense of responsibilities and thereby being better in expressing themselves. Thus, it can be said that at this higher level of education, trainees belonging to fathers with different occupational backgrounds do not differ in their level of assertiveness.

4.1.4: Parents Educational Status and Level of Assertiveness

Similar to income and occupation, educational status of parents also has potential of influencing level of assertiveness in behaviour of teachertrainees. In this context, comparison of level of assertiveness in behaviour of trainees belonging to fathers and mothers of different educational strata was carried out. Table 4.5.0, Fig.4.4 and Table 4.5.1 present result of analysis carried out in the context of educational status of father, while Table 4.6.0, Fig. 4.5 and Table 4.6.1 present findings obtained through the analysis carried out in the context of mother's educational status.

Table 4.5.0: Comparison of Level of Assertiveness among Teacher trainees belonging to Fathers with different Educational Status

Educational status	Number	Mean	Standard Deviation
Illiterate	7	194.28	30.68
Primary	25	190.88	26.55
Secondary	165	203.54	24.06
Graduation	107	204.44	22.27
Post graduation & Above	90	205.95	24.31

Table 4.5.1: Results of ANOVA of Assertiveness scores of Teacher trainees belonging to Fathers with different Educational Status

Source of variation	Sum of squares	Degree of freedom	Mean square	Fvalue	Significance at 0.05 level
Between groups	5206.74	4	1301.69	2.27	Not-Significant
Within groups	222735.15	389	572.58		
Total	227941.90	393			

An observation of Table 4.5.0 revealed that highest mean on assertiveness score (m=205.95) was associated with trainees whose fathers had an educational status of 'post graduation and above'. The next higher level of mean assertiveness score (m=204.44) was associated with trainees whose fathers had obtained education up to 'graduation' level. Teachertrainees belonging to fathers with secondary level of education were found to be 203.54, whereas mean score obtained by trainees belonging to fathers either illiterate or educated up to primary level only was observed to be more or less equal, being represented by respective means of 194.28 and 190.88. Trainees belonging to fathers in 'illiterate' and 'primary'

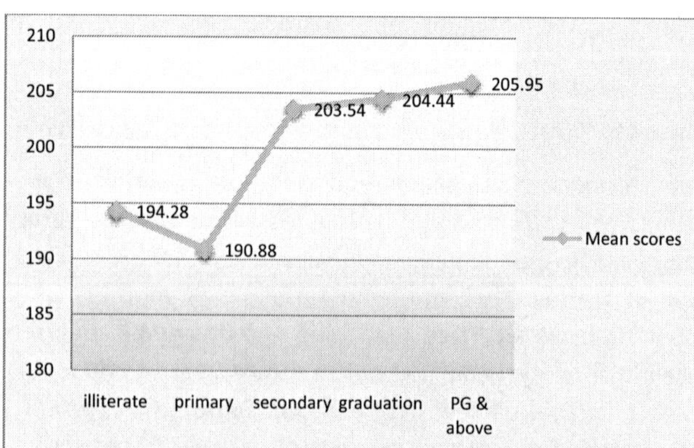

Figure 4.4: Mean scores obtained by Respondents belonging to Fathers with different Educational Status

educational groups appear to be lower in assertiveness as compared to the other three educational groups. However, results of analysis of variance shown in Table- 4.5.1 revealed that father's educational status did not interact with level of assertiveness of trainees.

Table 4.6.0: Comparison of Level of Assertiveness among Teacher trainees belonging to Mothers with different Educational Status

Educational status	Number	Mean	Standard Deviation
Illiterate	44	194.00	31.52
Primary	126	202.98	20.68
Secondary	168	204.42	23.39
Graduation	30	210.20	23.04
Post graduation & Above	26	206.50	27.78

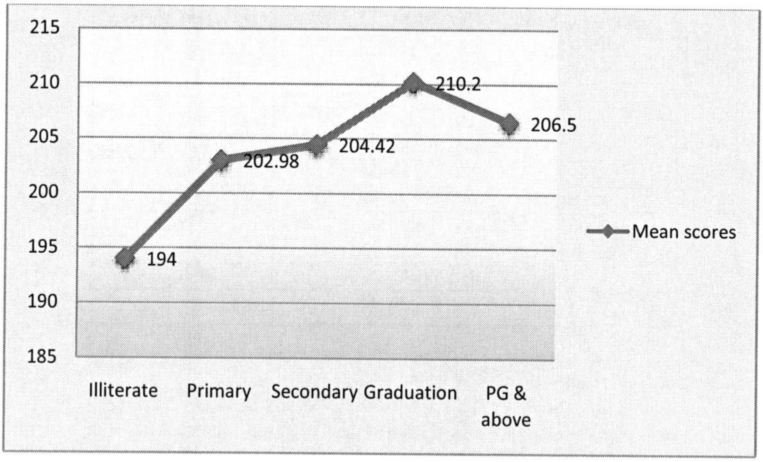

Figure 4.5: Mean scores obtained by Respondents belonging to Mothers with different Educational Status

It is indicated in Table 4.6.0 that higher means on assertiveness scores (m=210.20) and (m=206.50) were associated with trainees whose mothers were educated to graduation, post graduation and above levels respectively (Fig.4.5). The next higher level of mean assertiveness score (m=204.42) was associated with trainees whose mothers had obtained education up to 'secondary' level. Teacher-trainees belonging to mothers with primary level of education were found to be 202.98, whereas mean score obtained by trainees belonging to illiterate mothers was observed to be 194.00. Trainees belonging to mothers in 'illiterate' and 'primary' educational groups also appear to be lower in assertiveness as compared to the other three educational groups. Results of analysis of variance, shown in Table 4.6.1, revealed significant interaction between mother's educational status and level of assertiveness of trainees.

Table 4.6.1: Results of ANOVA of Assertiveness scores of Teacher trainees belonging to Mothers with different Educational Status

Source of variance	Sum of squares	Degree of freedom	Mean square	Fvalue	Significance at 0.05 level
Between groups	5720.84	4	1430.21		
Within groups	222221.06	389	571.26	2.50	Significant
Total	227941.90	393			

Table 4.6.2: Two-group Comparison on Assertiveness among Teacher-trainees belonging to Mothers with different Educational Status*

Two groups mean compared	Significance of mean difference at .05 level	Direction of mean difference
m_1-m_2	Significant	$m_1 < m_2$
m_1-m_3	Significant	$m_1 < m_3$
m_1-m_4	Significant	$m_1 < m_4$
m_1-m_5	Significant	$m_1 < m_5$
m_2-m_3	not- significant	$m_2 < m_3$
m_2-m_4	not- significant	$m_2 < m_4$
m_2-m_5	not- significant	$m_2 < m_5$
m_3- m_4	not- significant	$m_3 < m_4$
m_3- m_5	not- significant	$m_3 < m_5$
m_4- m_5	not- significant	$m_4 > m_5$

*m_1 = mean of trainees belonging to 'illiterate' mothers
m_2 = mean of trainees belonging to mothers educated to 'primary' level
m_3 = mean of trainees belonging to mothers educated to 'secondary' level
m_4 = mean of trainees belonging to mothers educated to 'graduation' level
m_5 = mean of trainees belonging to mothers educated to 'post-graduation' level

Table 4.6.2 present two group comparisons on assertiveness among teacher- trainees belonging to mothers educated to different levels.

Table 4.6.1 indicated presence of statistically significant differences between some of the groups of trainees belonging to mothers educated to different levels. Post-hoc comparisons between mother's education groups revealed that level of assertiveness among trainees belonging to mothers in 'illiterate' group was significantly lower than level of assertiveness among trainees belonging to mothers in 'primary', 'secondary', 'graduation' and 'post graduation' levels of education. These Post-hoc test also revealed that there was no significant difference in the level of assertiveness among trainees belonging to mothers educated up to 'primary', 'secondary', 'graduation' and 'post graduation' level groups. Findings of the present study brought-forth the fact that teacher-trainees belonging to 'illiterate mothers' were significantly different than teachertrainees belonging to mothers with other educational status group. Mothers' being educated, thus, seems to shape the level of assertiveness of their daughters.

In this context, findings obtained by Mentes (2007) are pertinent, which show that both father's and mother's educational status have a bearing on the level of assertiveness of their children. Mueen et. al. (2006) and Ibrahim (2015) have also revealed significant relationship in assertiveness and educational status of parents. Contrary to this, Gangwar (2012) in his study on secondary school students found that level of assertive behaviour is not influenced by educational status of parents. Findings of present study, however, indicate that in Indian settings and in the case of female teacher-trainees, it is mother's educational status only which influences ward's assertiveness.

4.1.5: Academic Achievement and Level of Assertiveness

One of the important objectives of present study was to find out the nature of interaction between assertiveness and academic achievement among teacher-trainees from different training institutions. The indicator of academic achievement was taken to be percentage of marks obtained by teacher-trainees in the final examination of the qualifying class. The frequency distribution of percentage of marks obtained by respondents is presented in Table 4.7.0.

Table 4.7.0: Distribution of Marks obtained by Respondents of the Sample

Class interval	Frequency	Percent (%)	Statistical indices
75-79	02	0.6	mean = 56.69
70-74	21	5.3	median = 55.90
65-69	28	7.1	mode = 50.00
60-64	57	14.5	SD = 6.56
55-59	125	31.7	minimum=40.00
50-54	138	35.0	maximum=78.65
45-49	16	4.1	Q1 = 52.00
40-44	07	1.8	Q3 = 60.00
Total	394	100	

It may be observed from Table 4.7.0 that the range of marks varied from 40 percent to 78.65 percent, while the median lied at the value of 55.90. The average achievement of teacher-trainees was represented by a mean value of 56.69 only. Three sub-groups of female teacher-trainees were identified on the basis of Q1 (52%) and Q3 (60%) values. One hundred and five female trainees belonged to the low academic achievement group (52% & below), while 104 trainees belonged to high academic achievement group (60 % & above). A majority of 185 trainees belonged to average academic achievement group. An observation of Table 4.8.0 and 4.8.1 reveals that mean value on assertiveness scores attained higher level in the average and high academic achievement group as compared to the group lower in academic achievement (See also Fig.4.6).

Table 4.8.0: Comparison of Level of Assertiveness among Teacher trainees with different Academic Achievement Status

Academic achievement status	Number	Mean	Standard Deviation
Low academic achievement group (52 percent and below)	105	201.35	21.37
Average academic achievement group (53 percent to 59 percent)	185	204.00	24.57
High academic achievement group (60 percent and above)	104	204.28	25.84

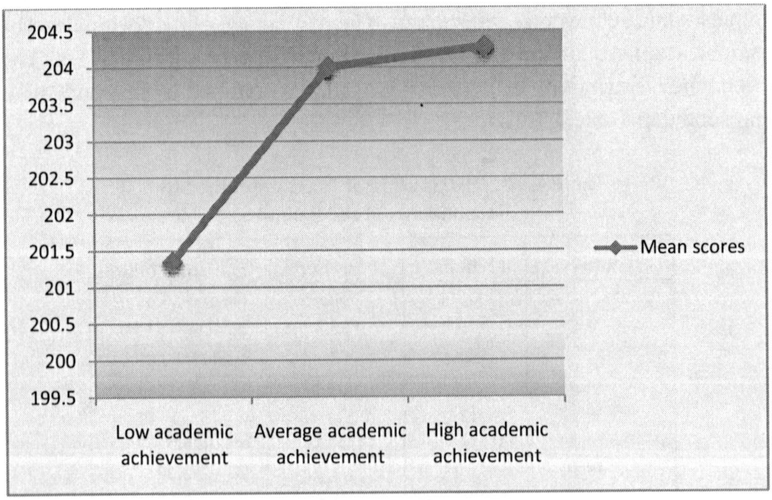

Figure 4.6: Mean scores obtained by Respondents with different Academic Achievement Status

Table 4.8.1: Results of ANOVA of Assertiveness scores of Teacher trainees with different Academic Achievement Status

Source of variation	Sum of squares	Degree of freedom	Mean square	F-value	Significance at 0.05 level
Between groups	588.03	2	294.01	0.51	Not-Significant
Within groups	227353.87	391	581.47		
Total	227941.90	393			

It is indicated in Table 4.8.1 that results obtained through analysis of variance of assertiveness scores of teacher-trainees belonging to different academic achievement status yielded a non-significant F-value at 0.05 level of significance. Here, findings revealed that level of academic attainment does not have a significant influence on level of assertiveness among teacher-trainees. Similarly in Indian context, results obtained by Gangwar (2012) showed no interaction between assertive behaviour and academic achievement. Beaver (1987) also indicated that assertive behaviour training did not reveal any significant change in academic achievement after the intervention among students enrolled in a vocational nursing programme. Similar findings were obtained on female secondary students of Iran by Paeezy, et. al. (2010). On the other hand, Rodriquez et. al. (2001), in a study on assertiveness among Hispanic college women, found significant differences in assertiveness level of groups based on academic classification. It was also revealed by Moon (2009) that academic assertiveness is required to attain academic and professional success.

4.2.0: Comparison of Posttest Means on Assertiveness, Self-Acceptance and Academic Achievement Motivation among Female Teacher-trainees belonging to Control and Experimental groups.

Analysis of effect of assertiveness training on different dependent variables was done by comparing posttest means of scores obtained by trainees of control group on selected variables with the posttest mean of scores obtained by trainees of the experimental group after the intervention. These posttest scores were obtained by administrating the tools which were used previously on trainees of the two groups at pretest stage. In this manner, comparison of posttest scores was sensitive to the effects of assertiveness training programme on selected variables of trainees in the experimental group. Table 4.9.1 and related Figure 4.7 presents comparison of posttest mean scores obtained by teacher-trainees belonging to control and experimental groups.

Table 4.9.1: Comparison of Posttest Means on Assertiveness among Teacher-trainees belonging to Control and Experimental groups

Institution Group	Number	Mean	Standard Deviation	t-value	Significance at 0.05 level
Control	35	210.20	23.15	5.22	Significant
Experimental	35	239.66	24.06		

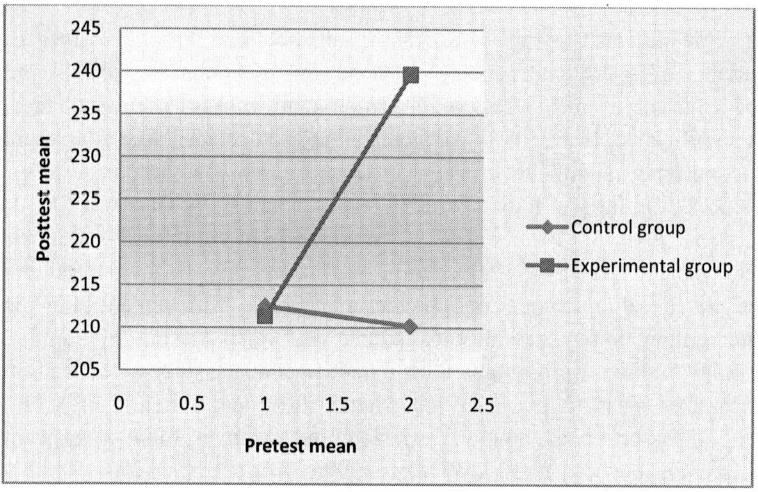

Figure 4.7: Pretest and Posttest Mean scores on Assertiveness obtained by Respondents of Control and Experimental groups

An observation of Table 4.9.1 revealed that trainees of experimental group, who have undergone assertiveness training, have scored higher mean on assertiveness (239.66) than the mean (210.20) scored by trainees in the control group, who were not given any such training. The difference between two means was found to be significant at 0.05 level, which indicates that the training given to individuals in experimental group was effective in increasing their level of assertiveness (See also Fig.4.7). This finding can be attributed to the fact that implementation of assertiveness training in experimental group provided trainees with opportunities and situations to participate and express their opinions and feelings along with encouraging them to resolve challenging situations.

Training programme based on a range of behavioural and cognitive methods and procedures using techniques of modeling, role playing, feedback, reinforcement, collective small and large group discussions, rehearsals, use of 'I' statements, use of assertive body language and home assignments, resulted in modification of behavioural components of trainees in an assertive manner. The well framed components of 'self awareness', 'awareness of rights', 'refining goals', 'feeling talk', 'awareness of reasons for nonassertion', 'ability to handle putdowns', 'awareness of one's body language', 'developing assertive body language', 'being able to say 'no', 'being able to make requests', 'skill of handling conflicts', 'ability to identify stereotypes', and 'handling discrepant situations' helped in raising assertiveness level among trainees.

Thus, results of the present study are in congruence with number of researches which investigated the effect of assertiveness training in different populations. Studies conducted by Grant and Devorah (1980); Rotheram and Armstrong (1980); Rotheram, et. al.(1982); Lee and Crockett (1994); Firth (2001); Sert (2003); Lina, et. al. (2004); Flowers (2006); Rezan (2009) Kashani and Bayat (2010); Tavakoli et.al. (2014), and Abed, et.al. (2015) found that assertiveness training was effective in improving assertiveness. The findings of present study establish truth of this in the population of female teacher-trainees.

Posttest means on self-acceptance, obtained by trainees of control and experimental groups are compared in Table 4.9.2 and Figure 4.8.

Table 4.9.2: Comparison of Posttest Means on Self-Acceptance among Teacher-trainees belonging to Control and Experimental groups

Institution Group	Number	Mean	Standard Deviation	t-value	Significance at 0.05 level
Control	35	16.57	2.52	4.66	Significant
Experimental	35	19.68	3.05		

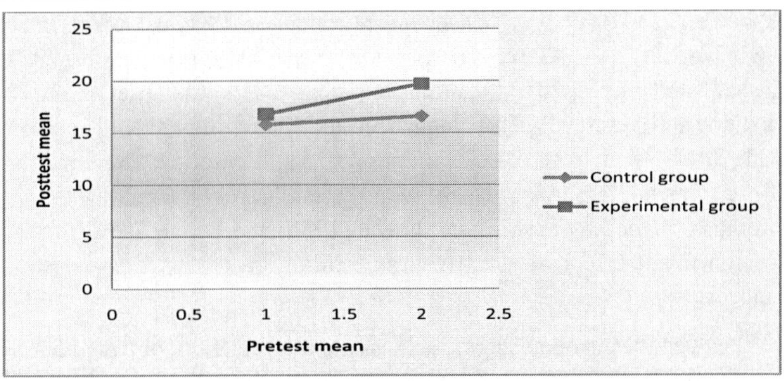

Figure 4.8: Pretest and Posttest Mean scores on Self-Acceptance obtained by Respondents of Control and Experimental groups

It may be observed from Table 4.9.2 and Figure 4.8 that trainees from the experimental group have scored higher mean on level of selfacceptance (19.68) than the mean (16.57) scored by trainees in control group. The difference between two means was found to be significant at 0.05 level, which indicates that assertiveness training given to individuals in the experimental group was effective in enhancing level of selfacceptance among teacher trainees of experimental group. The results obtained in the present study indicate effectiveness of assertiveness training in improving self-acceptance among female teacher-trainees. Self acceptance has been viewed to be the second pillar of self-esteem by Branden (1995), who reported self assertiveness as an essential component of self-esteem. Therefore increase in assertiveness leads to an increase in self-esteem or the component related to self. Moreover, assertiveness training focuses not only on explanation of concepts of behaviour and personality types (aggressive, assertive and non-assertive), overt behaviours (body language, expressions of feeling and opinions) and social interactions (giving compliments, identification of stereotypes, handling putdowns, conflicts and discrepant situations), but also on the thought processes (self-awareness, awareness of rights, awareness of reasons of non-assertion, refining goals, nurturing self-esteem). Assertiveness training sessions provided participants with freedom, enthusiasm and openness to think, interact, role play and discuss in small and large group with continuous feedback and supportive atmosphere, and a safe respect for their beliefs on the part of researcher motivated trainees to accept themselves in their own ways.

A number of positive consequences of applying assertive techniques on components related to self have been noted by many researchers, which included perception of self, self-esteem, self-efficacy, confidence, selfconcept and level of self-acceptance (Leman, 1998; Stake & Pearlman, 1980; Kazdin, 1982; Gupta, et. al., 2002 ; Sert, 2003; Lina, et. al., 2004; Kashani and Bayat, 2010; Makhija & Singh, 2010; Akbari,et.al., 2012; Makinde and Akinteye, 2014; Noghabaee and Nikoogoftar, 2014; Tavakoli, et.al., 2014; Abed, et.al., 2015; Tannous, 2015 and Yusefi, 2015). Findings of present study are in agreement with these researches. Contrary to this, findings obtained by Stewart and Lewis (1986) and Beaver (1987) found no significant effect of assertiveness training on selfesteem and self–concept.

Posttest means on academic achievement motivation, obtained by the trainees of control and experimental groups are shown in Table 4.9.3 and Figure 4.9.

Table 4.9.3: Comparison of Posttest Means on Academic Achievement Motivation among Teacher-trainees belonging to Control and Experimental groups

Institution Group	Number	Mean	Standard Deviation	t-value	Significance at 0.05 level
Control	35	31.03	3.01	0.91	Not-Significant
Experimental	35	31.68	3.03		

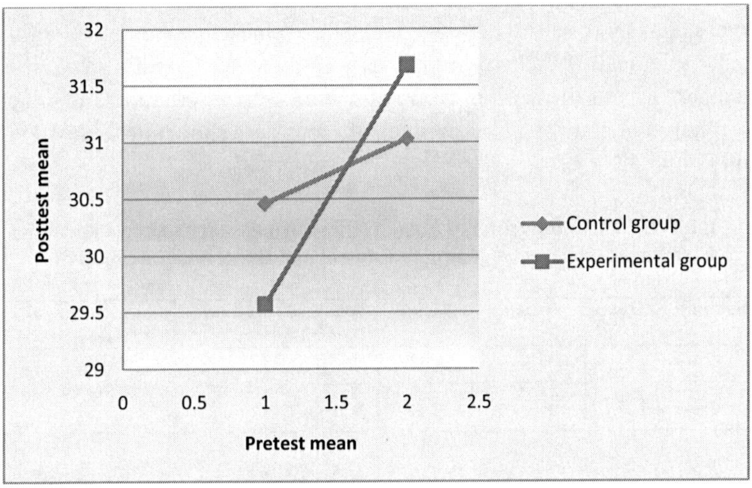

Figure 4.9: Pretest and Posttest Mean scores on Academic Achievement Motivation obtained by Respondents of Control and Experimental groups

Table 4.9.3 indicated that posttest mean score on level of academic achievement motivation (31.68) obtained by trainees of experimental group was slightly higher than posttest mean (31.03) score of trainees in control group. The difference between two means was not found to be significant at 0.05 level, which indicates that assertive training given to individuals in the experimental group did not help in increasing their level of academic achievement motivation in a significant way (See also Fig.4.9). The present findings support previous researches that obtained no significant difference on academic achievement through assertiveness training (Beaver, 1987; Makhija & Singh, 2010; Paeezy, et. al. 2010; and Yusefi, 2015). On the other hand, findings obtained by Rotheram, et. al.,1982; Mansur, 2007; and Ashouri, 2008 revealed positive effect of assertiveness training on the measure of academic achievement. A better understanding of this aspect needs to be generated through further analysis of data.

4.3.0: Comparison of Mean Gain scores on Assertiveness, Self-Acceptance and Academic Achievement Motivation among Teacher-trainees belonging to Control and Experimental groups

In order to make the analysis of effect of assertiveness training on different dependent variables more sensitive to input status of participants of experiment, it was considered more suitable to compute gain scores on different dependent variables. These gain scores were derived through subtracting pre-test score of each individual from her post-test scores on a particular variable. In this manner, comparison of gain scores at post-test level seems more sensitive to the direction of changes taking place within each individual of the two groups, as well as to the overall direction of changes in both the groups.Mean gain scores on assertiveness obtained by trainees of control and experimental groups are shown in Table 4.10.1 and Figure 4.10.

Table 4.10.1: Comparison of Mean Gain scores on Assertiveness among Teacher-trainees belonging to Control and Experimental groups

Institution Group	Number	Mean	Standard Deviation	t-value	Significance at 0.05 level
Control	35	-2.37	20.23	5.46	Significant
Experimental	35	28.28	26.30		

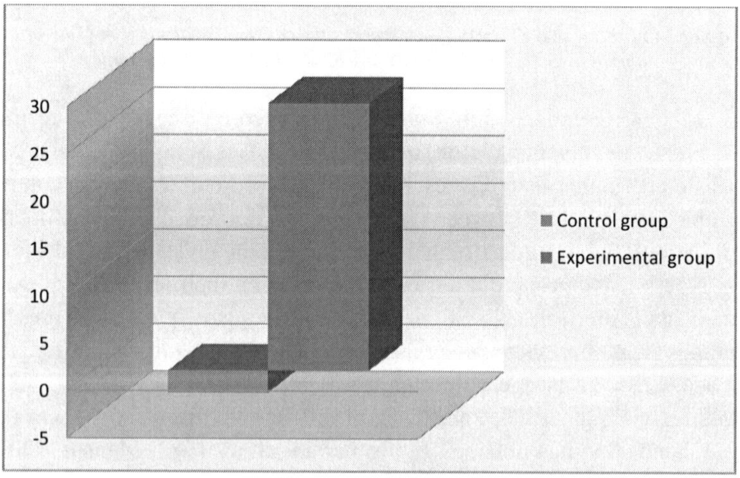

Figure 4.10: Mean scores on Gain in Assertiveness obtained by Respondents of Control and Experimental groups

Table 4.10.1. and Figure 4.10 revealed that mean of gain scores on assertiveness in experimental group (28.28), computed by subtracting the pre-test score obtained by each trainee on the same variable from her posttest score, was comparatively higher than mean of gain scores (m=-2.37) obtained by trainees in the control group. The t-value (5.46) was found to be significant at 0.05 level, which indicates that level of assertiveness amon teacher-trainees of experimental group has significantly increased. Here, mean value (-) 2.37 of gain scores on assertiveness in the control group also indicated that level of assertiveness among trainees in the control group had slightly decreased. It may be pointed out that there was a period of four months between the pretest and posttest, and pretest was conducted by the researcher in both control and experimental groups when female teacher-trainees were fresh to B.Ed. course. Then, with the advent of time and facing the technicalities of the course, female teacher-trainees developed anxiety towards career and life, which may have resulted in decrease in assertiveness among teacher-trainees of control group. Assertiveness training provided in the experimental group, on the other hand, may be viewed as considerably helping trainees in overcoming their anxiety and becoming more assertive in dealing with the requirements of B.Ed. course and living consciously.

A comparison of gain scores on self-acceptance, attained by teachertrainees of control and experimental groups is presented in Table 4.10.2 and Figure 4.11., while comparison of mean of gain scores on academic achievement motivation among trainees of the two groups is shown in Table 4.10.3 and related Figure 4.12.

Table 4.10.2: Comparison of Mean of Gain scores on Self-Acceptance among Teacher-trainees belonging to Control and Experimental groups

Institution Group	Number	Mean	Standard Deviation	t-value	Significance at 0.05 level
Control	35	0.80	3.06	2.52	Significant
Experimental	35	2.91	3.91		

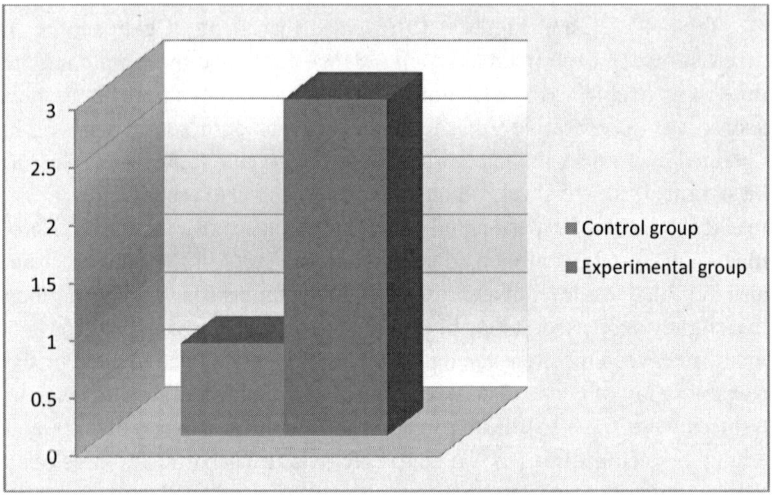

Figure 4.11: Mean scores on Gain in Self-Acceptance obtained by Respondents of Control and Experimental groups

Table 4.10.3: Comparison of Gain scores on Academic Achievement Motivation among Teacher-trainees belonging to Control and Experimental groups

Institution Group	Number	Mean	Standard Deviation	t-value	Significance at 0.05 level
Control	35	0.57	2.85	2.42	Significant
Experimental	35	2.11	2.47		

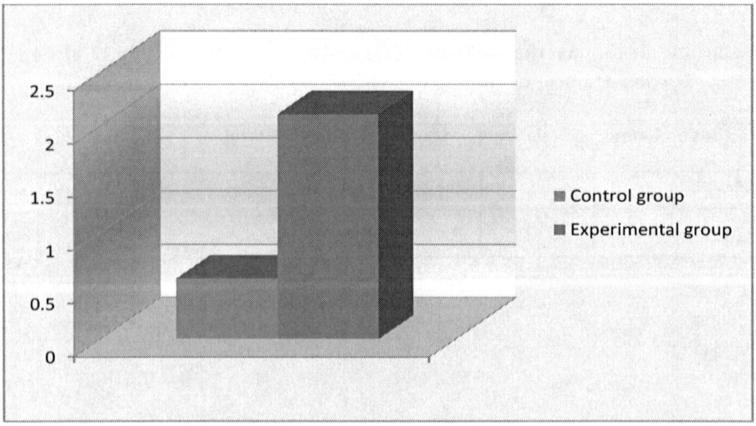

Figure 4.12: Mean scores on Gain in Academic Achievement Motivation obtained by Respondents of Control and Experimental groups

It is evident from Table 4.10.2 and Table 4.10.3 that trainees belonging to experimental group have higher mean gain scores on level of self-acceptance (m=2.91) and level of (m=2.11) than mean gain scores obtained by trainees of control group. Gains in level of self-acceptance and academic achievement motivation among trainees of experimental group were found to be significantly high in comparison to control group, which indicates that training in assertiveness provided to teacher-trainees in experimental group was effective in raising the levels of self-acceptance and academic achievement motivation among trainees in a significant way (See also Fig-4.11 and Fig-4.12).

Findings related to increase in level of self-acceptance among teacher-trainees after receiving assertiveness training is interpreted earlier in section 4.2.0. However, different findings related to significant gain in academic achievement motivation level of trainees of experimental group obtained in this analysis can be interpreted on the ground that experimental group trainees did not differ significantly from control group trainees in their academic achievement motivation levels at posttest due to the reason that trainees of control group were candidates who have attained higher scores in B.Ed. entrance examination, and therefore secured admission in university campus on free seat (comparatively less amount of admission fees), while trainees of experimental group were relatively lower in entrance scores.

Since posttest was carried out after a period of four months and conduction of assertiveness training in experimental group, it can be stated that motivation level of experimental group trainees for academic achievement received significant gain, as assertiveness training helped participants in developing their understanding of 'self' and their 'needs' along with providing them skills of communication and expression in an assertive manner so that their motivation to gain academic achievement has increased in a positive manner, whereas trainees of control group did not received any such motivation through regular B.Ed. programme. Therefore, difference in mean of gain scores was found to be significant, indicating efficacy of assertiveness training in increasing academic achievement motivation of female teacher-trainees in a significant manner.

4.4.0: Comparison of Effect of Assertiveness Training on Posttest scores on Assertiveness within Sub-groups identified on the basis of Socio-demographic Characteristics

In the analysis carried out in section 4.1, the investigator attempted to identify different characteristics of trainees that interact with their level of assertiveness in a significant way. This analysis revealed that the caste group membership, family income, occupation carried out by fathers, father's educational status and academic achievement characteristics do not interact significantly with level of assertiveness shown by trainees. Mother's educational status was, however, found to influence level of assertiveness among female teacher-trainees in a significant manner. The mean scores obtained by female teacher-trainees belonging to General caste, high income group, belonging to fathers engaged in 'teaching' occupation and educated up to 'higher education' level and with higher academic achievement were found to be somewhat higher on level of assertiveness. Findings described in section 4.2 and 4.3 revealed statistically significant differences in control and experimental groups on selected dependent variables after intervention.

In light of these findings, it was considered important to compare the effect of assertiveness training on level of assertiveness within experimental subgroups identified on the basis of socio-demographic and personal variables selected in the study. Subgroups identified within control group were also studied to compare level of assertiveness at posttest level, since respondents of control group were also getting inputs personality development through curriculum as regular trainees of a teacher education programme.

4.4.1: Comparison of Effect of Assertiveness Training on Posttest scores on Assertiveness within Subgroups identified on the basis of Caste

It may be noted that female teacher-trainees belonging to 'General' caste were found to be higher on assertiveness than those belonging to Other Backward Caste, Scheduled Caste and Scheduled Tribes groups. Therefore, caste membership of teacher-trainees was regrouped into two categories: 'General' and 'Others'. The experimental and control groups were, thus, viewed as consisted of two caste-based subgroups: 'General' and 'Others'. The effect of assertiveness training was analyzed within the experimental subgroups identified on the basis of caste. The subgroups identified within control group were also compared to test level of assertiveness. Findings obtained are shown in Tables-4.11.1 and 4.11.2 (See also Fig-4.13).

Table 4.11.1: Comparison of Posttest scores on Assertiveness within Control and Experimental Subgroups identified on the basis of Caste

Sub-groups	Number	Mean	Standard Deviation	F-value	Significance at 0.05 level
Control group- 'General' Caste	24	210.21	26.33		
Control group- 'Others' Caste	11	210.18	15.05		
Experimental group- 'General' Caste	26	237.58	21.82	9.17	Significant
Experimental group- 'Others' Caste	09	245.67	30.30		

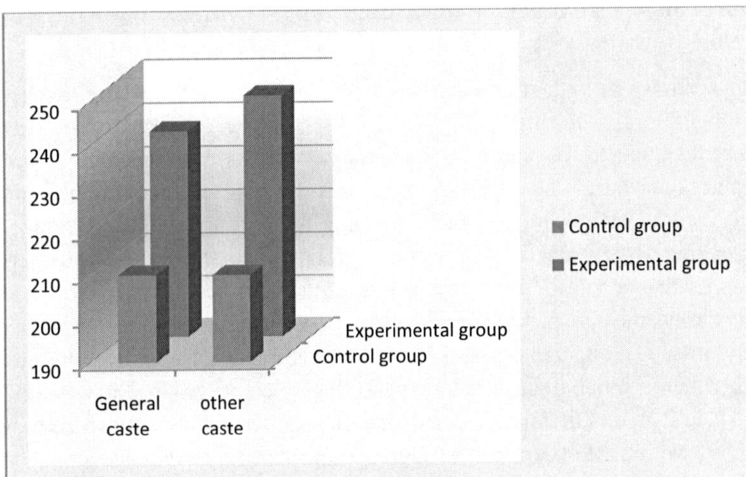

Figure 4.13: Posttest scores on Assertiveness obtained by Respondents of Control and Experimental Subgroups identified on the basis of Caste

Table 4.11.2: Two-group Comparison of Posttest scores on Assertiveness within Control and Experimental Subgroups identified on the basis of Caste

Two groups compared	Significance of mean difference at .05 level	Direction of mean difference
$m_1 - m_2$	not-significant	$m_1 > m_2$
$m_3 - m_4$	not- significant	$m_3 < m_4$

*m_1 = mean of control group trainees belonging to 'General' caste

m_2 = mean of control group trainees belonging to 'Others' caste

m_3 = mean of experimental group trainees belonging to 'General' caste

m_4 = mean of experimental group trainees belonging to 'Others' caste

An observation of Tables-4.11.1, 4.11.2 and Figure 4.13 indicated that mean score on assertiveness obtained by control group trainees belonging to two different caste groups was more or less similar, whereas the level of assertiveness in experimental group trainees belonging to 'Others' caste group was higher than 'General' caste teacher-trainees. The Post-hoc tests, however, revealed no significant difference in level of assertiveness among 'General' and 'Others' caste trainees within control and experimental groups. Findings of present analysis, thus, revealed that the effect of assertiveness training was significant on assertiveness level of trainees of both 'General' and 'Others' caste groups.

4.4.2: Comparison of Effect of Assertiveness Training on Posttest scores on Assertiveness within Subgroups identified on the basis of Family income

Findings described in section 4.1 have revealed that teacher-trainees belonging to 'high income' group were somewhat higher on mean assertiveness score than trainees belonging to 'low income' and 'average income' groups. Trainees in control and experimental groups were, therefore, regrouped into two income categories: trainees belonging to 'high income' and trainees belonging to 'low and average income' groups. Four subgroups of teacher-trainees thus identified were: control group trainees belonging to 'low and average income' group, control group trainees belonging to 'high income' group, experimental group trainees belonging to 'low and average income' group and experimental group trainees belonging to 'high income' group. Tables-4.12.1 and 4.12.2 present findings obtained through analysis of effect of assertiveness training within the experimental subgroups and analysis carried out within the subgroups of control group (See also Fig-4.14).

Table 4.12.1: Comparison of Posttest scores on Assertiveness within Control and Experimental Subgroups identified on the basis of Family income

Sub-groups	Number	Mean	Standard deviation	F-value	Significance at 0.05 level
Control group- 'low and average' income	25	213.00	22.11	9.49	Significant
Control group- 'high' income	10	203.20	25.38		
Experimental group- 'low and average' income	24	238.33	23.59		
Experimental group- 'high' income	11	242.54	26.00		

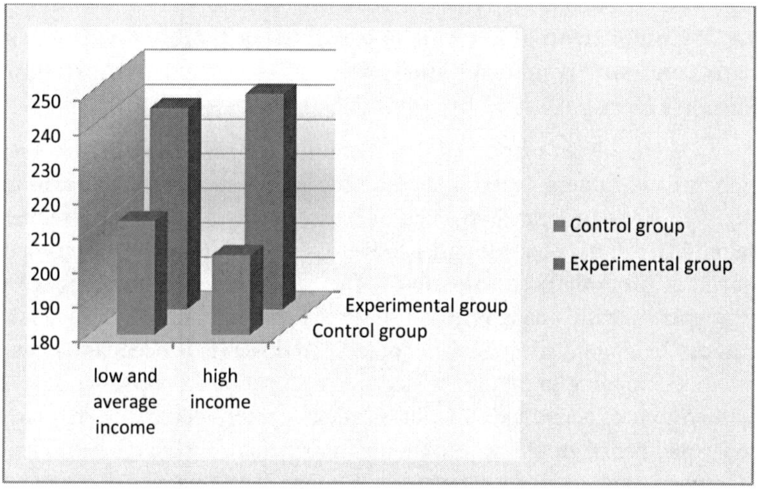

Figure 4.14: Posttest scores on Assertiveness obtained by Respondents of Control and Experimental Subgroups identified on the basis of Family income

Table 4.12.2: Two-group Comparison of Posttest scores on Assertiveness within Control and Experimental Subgroups identified on the basis of Family income

Two groups compared	Significance of mean difference at .05 level	Direction of mean difference
m_1- m_2	not-significant	$m_1 > m_2$
m_3- m_4	not- significant	$m_3 < m_4$

*m_1 = mean of control group trainees belonging to 'low and average' income families

m_2 = mean of control group trainees belonging to 'high' income families

m_3 = mean of experimental group trainees belonging to 'low and average' income families

m_4 = mean of experimental group trainees belonging to 'high' income families

It is highlighted in Tables- 4.12.1, 4.12.2 and Figure 4.14 that the subgroup of teacher-trainees belonging to 'high' income group in experimental group have scored higher mean on assertiveness in comparison to 'low and average' income group, whereas teacher-trainees belonging to 'low and average' income group were found to attain higher level of assertiveness than trainees belonging to 'high' income group in control group. Post-hoc comparisons, however, revealed no significant difference in level of assertiveness within control and experimental subgroups. Findings of present analysis, thus, revealed that assertiveness training was significantly and equally effective in increasing level of assertiveness in experimental subgroups identified on the basis of family income.

4.4.3: Comparison of Effect of Assertiveness Training on Posttest scores on Assertiveness within Subgroups identified on the basis of Father's Occupation

In the analysis carried out in section 4.1, female teacher-trainees belonging to fathers engaged in 'teaching' occupation were found to be slightly higher on mean associated with assertiveness scores than trainees belonging to fathers working as 'government employee' or engaged in 'farming' or 'others' occupations. Therefore, teacher- trainees were regrouped into two categories on the basis of their father's occupation: trainees belonging to fathers in 'others' (non-service) occupations and trainees belonging to fathers in 'service' occupations. Four subgroups of teacher-trainees, identified on the bases of their father's occupation in control and experimental groups, were (i) control group trainees belonging to fathers in 'others' (non-service) occupations, (ii) control group trainees belonging to fathers in 'service' occupations, (iii) experimental group trainees belonging to fathers in 'others' (non-service) occupations and (iv) experimental group trainees belonging to fathers in 'service' occupations. The effect of assertiveness training was analyzed within these subgroups and findings obtained are shown in Tables-4.13.1, 4.13.2 and related Figure 4.15.

Table 4.13.1: Comparison of Posttest scores on Assertiveness within Control and Experimental Subgroups identified on the basis of Father's Occupation

Sub-groups	Number	Mean	Standard deviation	F-value	Significance at 0.05 level
Control group- fathers in 'others' (nonservice) occupation	11	206.64	18.96		
Control group- fathers in 'service' occupation	24	211.83	25.04		
Experimental group- fathers in 'others' (nonservice) occupation	13	240.15	18.41	8.98	Significant
Experimental group- fathers in 'service' occupation	22	239.36	27.27		

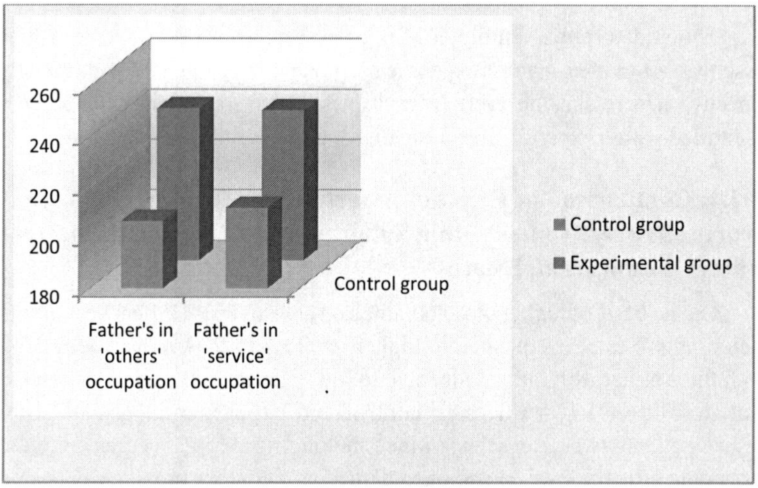

Figure 4.15: Posttest scores on Assertiveness obtained by Respondents of Control and Experimental Subgroups identified on the basis of Father's Occupation

Table 4.13.2: Two-group Comparison of Posttest scores on Assertiveness within Control and Experimental Subgroups identified on the basis of Father's Occupation

Two groups compared	Significance of mean difference at .05 level	Direction of mean difference
m_1- m_2	not-significant	$m_1 < m_2$
m_3- m_4	not- significant	$m_3 > m_4$

*m_1 = mean of control group trainees belonging to fathers in 'others' (non-service) occupations

m_2 = mean of control group trainees belonging to fathers in 'service' occupations

m_3 = mean of experimental group trainees belonging to fathers in 'others' (nonservice) occupations

m_4 = mean of experimental group trainees belonging to fathers in 'service' occupations

It may be observed from Tables-4.13.1, 4.13.2 and Figure 4.15 that the subgroup of teacher-trainees in control group belonging to fathers engaged in 'service' occupations have obtained somewhat higher scores on assertiveness than teacher-trainees belonging to fathers engaged in 'others' occupations. On the other hand, level of assertiveness was found to be almost similar in subgroups identified in the experimental group even after receiving training in assertiveness. Post-hoc comparisons also revealed no significant difference in the level of assertiveness among trainees belonging to fathers engaged in 'others' and 'service' occupations within the control and experimental groups. Findings of present analysis, thus, revealed that assertiveness training given in experimental group was significantly and similarly effective in increasing the level of assertiveness in two groups of teacher-trainees identified within experimental group on the basis of father's occupation.

4.4.4: Comparison of Effect of Assertiveness Training on Posttest scores on Assertiveness within Subgroups identified on the basis of Father's Educational Status

On the basis of higher mean obtained on assertiveness by teachertrainees belonging to fathers educated to higher levels than the trainees belonging to fathers either illiterate or educated to lower levels in the analysis carried out in section 4.1, trainees in control and experimental groups were regrouped into two categories: trainees belonging to fathers either illiterate or having primary level education and trainees belonging to fathers educated higher than primary level. Four subgroups of teachertrainees thus identified were ((i) Control group trainees belonging to fathers either illiterate or educated up to primary level (ii) Control group trainees belonging to fathers educated higher than primary level (iii) Experimental group trainees belonging to fathers either illiterate or educated up to primary level, and (iv) Experimental group trainees belonging to fathers educated higher than primary level. The following Tables-4.14.1, 4.14.2 and Figure 4.16 present analysis carried out to assess the effect of assertiveness training, and findings obtained in these subgroups.

Table 4.14.1: Comparison of Posttest scores on Assertiveness within Control and Experimental Subgroups identified on the basis of Father's Educational Status

Sub-groups	Number	Mean	Standard deviation	F-value	Significance at 0.05 level
Control group-fathers either'illiterate' or educated up to 'primary' level	05	198.80	18.03	11.33	Significant
Control group-fathers educated higher than 'primary' level	30	212.10	23.60		
Experimental group-fathers ' illiterate' or educated up to 'primary' level	03	265.00	9.54		
Experimental group-fathers educated higher than 'primary' level	32	237.28	23.69		

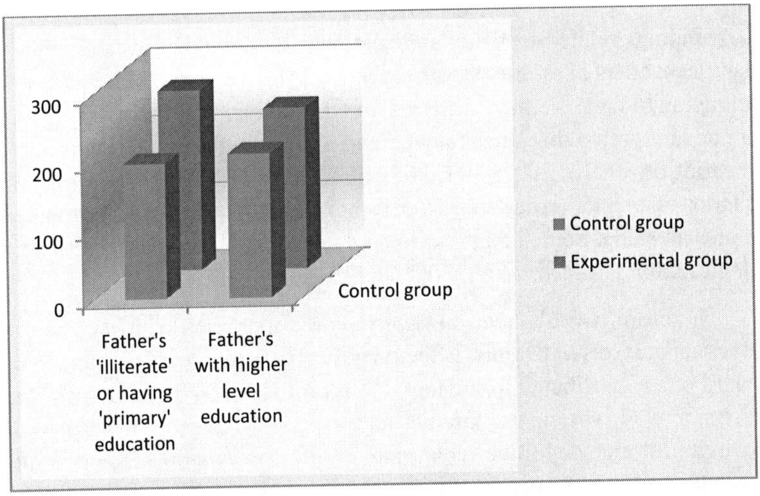

Figure 4.16: Posttest scores on Assertiveness obtained by Respondents of Control and Experimental Subgroups identified on the basis of Father's Education

Table 4.14.2: Two-group Comparison of Posttest scores on Assertiveness within Control and Experimental Subgroups identified on the basis of Father's Educational Status

Two groups compared	Significance of mean difference at .05 level	Direction of mean difference
$m_1 - m_2$	not-significant	$m_1 < m_2$
$m_3 - m_4$	significant	$m_3 > m_4$

*m_1 = mean of control group trainees belonging to fathers either 'illiterate or educated up to 'primary' level

m_2 = mean of control group trainees belonging to fathers educated higher than 'primary' level

m_3 = mean of experimental group trainees belonging to fathers either 'illiterate' or educated up to 'primary' level

m_4 = mean of experimental group trainees belonging to fathers educated higher than 'primary' level

It may be observed from Table 4.14.1 that the subgroup of teachertrainees belonging to fathers educated higher than primary level in the control group have slightly higher level of assertiveness than the teachertrainees belonging to fathers either 'illiterate' or educated up to 'primary' level. On the other hand, two group comparisons in Table 4.14.2 and Figure 4.16 revealed that the experimental group trainees belonging to fathers either 'illiterate' or educated up to 'primary' level have obtained significantly higher level of assertiveness in comparison to trainees belonging to fathers educated higher than 'primary' level.

Findings related to father's educational status, thus, revealed highly significant effect of assertiveness training on level of assertiveness of trainees belonging to fathers either 'illiterate' or educated up to primary level. This can be interpreted that since father's and mother's educational status have a bearing on level of assertiveness of their children. This fact is also justified in terms of interaction between assertiveness level of female teacher-trainees in present study. Some other researchers that revealed similar results were Mentes, 2007; Mueen, et. al., 2006 and Ibrahim, 2015.

Therefore, ward's level of assertiveness increases with increase in educational status of parents. Effectiveness of assertiveness training in this regard can be attributed to the fact that it provided equal opportunities to all trainees to participate, interact and express by means of a range of behavioural and cognitive techniques, with a provision of continuous feedback and focus on non-assertive ness helped trainees belonging to fathers with lower educational status to improve their assertiveness level in a significant manner.

4.4.5: Comparison of Effect of Assertiveness Training on Posttest scores on Assertiveness within Subgroups identified on the basis of Academic Achievement Status of Teacher-trainees

Analysis carried out in section 4.1 had revealed that teachertrainees with 'high' and 'average' academic achievement have attained somewhat higher level of assertiveness than the trainees belonging to 'low' academic achievement status. Therefore, trainees were regrouped into two categories on the basis of their academic achievement: trainees belonging to 'high and average' academic achievement and trainees belonging to 'low' achievement. Four subgroups of teacher-trainees thus identified, were

(i) Control group trainees with 'low' academic achievement

(ii) Control group trainees with 'average and high' academic achievement

(iii) Experimental group trainees with 'low' academic achievement and

(iv) Experimental group trainees with 'average and high' academic achievement. Effect of assertiveness training was analyzed within these subgroups and findings obtained are shown in Tables-4.15.1, 4.15.2 and Figure 4.17.

Table 4.15.1: Comparison of Posttest scores on Assertiveness within Control and Experimental Subgroups identified on the basis of Academic Achievement Status

Sub-groups	Number	Mean	Standard deviation	F-value	Significance at 0.05 level
Control group-'low' academic achievement	08	215.12	13.13	11.37	Significant
Control group-'average and high' academic	27	208.74	25.39		
Experimental group-'low' academic achievement	09	254.74	25.11		
Experimental group-'average and high' academic achievement	26	234.54	21.90		

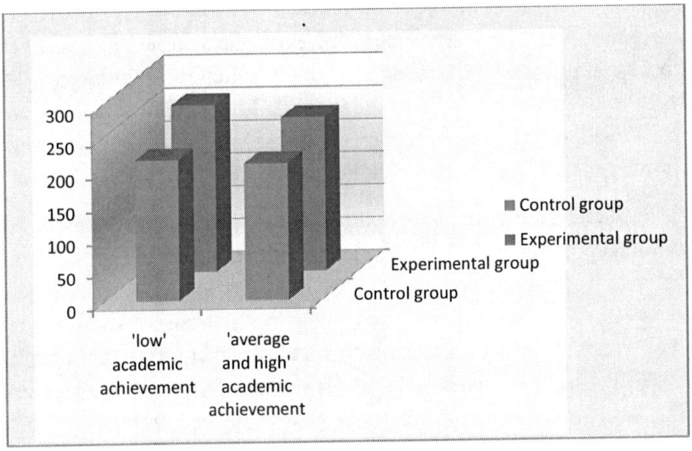

Figure 4.17: Posttest scores on Assertiveness obtained by Respondents of Control and Experimental Subgroups identified on the basis of Academic Achievement Status

Table 4.15.2: Two-group Comparison of Posttest scores on Assertiveness within Control and Experimental Subgroups identified on the basis of Academic Achievement Status

Two groups compared	Significance of mean difference at .05 level	Direction of mean difference
$m_1 - m_2$	not-significant	$m_1 > m_2$
$m_3 - m_4$	significant	$m_3 > m_4$

*m_1 = mean of control group trainees with 'low' academic achievement
m_2 = mean of control group trainees with 'average and high' academic achievement
m_3 = mean of experimental group trainees with 'low' academic achievement
m_4 = mean of experimental group trainees with 'average and high' academic achievement

It may be observed from Table 4.15.1, Table 4.15.2 and Figure 4.17 that although teacher-trainees with 'low' academic achievement in control group did not differ significantly from trainees belonging to 'average and high' academic achievement status, a significant difference was obtained within the experimental group trainees in terms of assertiveness. Teachertrainees with 'low' academic achievement were found to have attained significantly higher level of assertiveness than the trainees with 'average and high' academic achievement status after undergoing experiment.

Findings of present study, thus, indicated a highly significant effect of assertiveness training among trainees with 'low academic achievement' in experimental group. It can be concluded through present analysis that since academic assertiveness is required to attain academic and professional success (Moon, 2009) and significant differences are present in assertiveness level between groups based on academic classification (Rodriquez, et.al., 2001), assertiveness levels of trainees with 'low academic achievement' may be considered to have lower levels of assertiveness. This assumption was, however, not supported by findings of this study in earlier section 4.1.

Here, it can be stated that female teacher-trainees at this stage of their educational career continuously witness pressures of family for settlements in life, which may create hindrances in their academic progress and achievement. The intensity of such pressures increases when academic achievement is not up to satisfactory level. Such a situation contributes towards lowering assertive behaviour. Hence, effectiveness of assertiveness training was established in the sense that it helped trainees with 'low academic achievement' to develop an acceptance towards 'self' through encouraging assertive skills in dealing with day to day problems.

Chapter - 5

Findings and Conclusions of the Study

5.0.0 Findings, Conclusions and Implications of the Study

The design of the present study was prepared with specific aims and objectives in view. The overall research process of data collection and analysis was guided by these specific aims and objectives. Findings obtained through the analysis of the data can be synthesized into certain broad conclusions. The study also indicated certain implications for practice and further research. These various aspects constitute the content of present chapter, and are being described in following sections:

5.1.0 Summary

The significance of assertiveness training has been emphasized by a number of authors (Galassi, et. al.1974; Rotheram and Armstrong 1980; Buell and Snyder 1981; Kazdin and Mascitelli 1982; Rotheram, et. al.1982; Tanner and Holliman 1988; Lee and Crockett 1994; Firth 2001; Gupta, et. al. 2002; Kim 2003; Nota and Soresi 2003; Sert 2003; Lina, et. al. 2004; Flowers 2006; Rezan 2009; Tavakoli, et. al. 2009; Kashani and Bayat 2010; Nnodum 2010; Makhija & Singh 2010; Agbakwuru and Stella 2012; Akbari, et.al., 2012; Niusha, et.al., 2012; Asrowi and Barida, 2013; Babayi and Rahmati, 2014; Makinde and Akinteye, 2014; Noghabaee and Nikoogoftar, 2014; Tavakoli, et.al., 2014; Abed,et.al., 2015; Chinwe, 2015; Tannous, 2015; Yusefi, 2015 etc.)

It has been pointed out that training in assertiveness helps in increasing the level of assertiveness, improves self-esteem, helps in lowering stress, enhances social skills of even the isolates. It leads to significant increases in goal clarity, which in turn promotes ability to gather information for making choices, and, thus, improving level of decision making in addition to decrease in level of discomfort in social situations. Assertiveness training is also reported to be effective in case of indecisiveness. Improved level of self-concept, higher academic achievement, reduction in test anxiety and examination phobia, enhancement in progress motivation and higher popularity among students were also analyzed in groups that were given training in assertiveness.

Giving assertiveness training to children leads to acquisition of behaviours which are viewed as interpersonally effective and assertive, hence, enhancing social competency and interpersonal adjustment. Being a behaviour modification programme with such a wide range of implications, it emphasizes the need to undertake research on different facets of assertiveness training and its consequences on various aspects of life. In the field of education, it also puts an obvious demand for initiating more research activity to understand assertiveness training outcomes in different populations of students and teachers.

Present study was designed in view of this felt research need, and attempted to study the effect of assertiveness training programme on assertiveness, self-acceptance and academic achievement motivation among female teacher-trainees. More specifically, present study was designed to analyze and compare the level of assertiveness of female teacher-trainees across sub-groups identified on the basis of personal and socio-demographic characteristics and to study the effectiveness of a specifically designed assertiveness training programme on (i) level of assertiveness,(ii) level of self acceptance, and (iii) level of academic achievement motivation of female teacher-trainees. As a concomitant objective, the study also attempted to standardize a qualitative assertiveness questionnaire into an Assertive Behaviour Assessment Scale (ABAS) for teacher-trainees

A broad review of related research was undertaken to indicate different populations covered under the research effort initiated by earlier researchers, which pointed out effectiveness of assertiveness training programme in improving assertiveness and different desirable characteristics among the recipients of training. A review of different researches, exploring assertiveness as a function of individual's varied characteristics and research seeking to find out different correlates of assertiveness in behaviour was also carried out extensively. With the perspective provided by this broad review of research, following null hypotheses were proposed to be tested.

1. There is no significant difference in level of assertiveness among sub-groups of female teacher-trainees identified on the basis of their personal and socio-demographic characteristics:
   (i) Caste wise groups of female teacher-trainees do not differ in their level of assertiveness.
   (ii) Income wise groups of female teacher-trainees do not differ in their level of assertiveness.
   (iii) Groups of female teacher-trainees identified on the basis of occupational background of family do not differ in their level of assertiveness.
   (iv) Groups of female teacher-trainees identified on the basis of educational status of family do not differ in their level of assertiveness.
   (v) Academic achievement wise groups of female teacher-trainees do not differ in their level of assertiveness.
2. There is no significant effect of assertiveness training on level of assertiveness of female teacher-trainees.
3. There is no significant effect of assertiveness training on level of self-acceptance of female teacher-trainees.
4. There is no significant effect of assertiveness training on level of academic achievement motivation of female teacher-trainees.

   Additionally, at post-test stage the researcher proposed to test following hypotheses to explore the effect of assertiveness training on different groups of female teacher-trainees.
5. There is no significant differential effect of assertiveness training on level of assertiveness in groups of female teacher-trainees identified on the basis of :
   (vi) Caste
   (vii) Family income
   (viii) Occupational background of family
   (ix) Parent's educational status, and
   (x) Academic achievement

With reference to the above stated objectives, the overall research work was conducted in two stages i.e. (i) The Survey Stage and (ii) The Experimental Stage. Survey research method was adopted at the survey stage for the purpose of data collection and a sample of 394 female teacher-trainees of B.Ed. level were selected from eight institutions of Kumaun

University, Nainital through a multistage random sampling method. A specifically designed Personal Information Schedule (PIS) was used to collect information on different socio-demographic characteristics of teacher-trainees and their previous academic achievement. Assertive Behaviour Assessment Scale (ABAS), standardized by the researcher for B.Ed. level teacher-trainees, was used to assess the level of assertiveness. The data were collected in group situation within the institutions selected in the sample selection process.

The experimental research method was adopted at experimental stage to assess the effect of assertiveness training programme on level of assertiveness, self-acceptance and academic achievement motivation among teacher-trainees by employing Pretest- Posttest Equivalent-Groups Design, wherein two B.Ed. teacher training institutions were randomly selected for assigning to control and experimental group treatment. A group of thirty-five (35) subjects were randomly assigned to both experimental and control group. A test of statistical equivalence between control and experimental groups was carried out. The experimental group was provided assertiveness training by the investigator herself for a period of six days extended into twelve technical sessions. The pretest and posttest data were collected with the help of selected research tools from same group of trainees in both groups. Analysis of data in two stages was guided by the objectives of the study as well as the specific hypotheses proposed to be tested.

5.2.0 Findings of the Study

Findings of the study were directly related to the test of the null hypotheses proposed for the study. Therefore, the findings arrived may be summarized in accordance to the null hypotheses proposed to be tested in following manner-

Hypothesis-1: There is no significant difference in level of assertiveness among the sub-groups of female teacher-trainees identified on the basis of their personal and socio-demographic characteristics:

(i) Caste wise groups of female teacher-trainees do not differ in their level of assertiveness.

This hypothesis was tested for the overall group of female teachertrainees. It was found that the null hypothesis was true and there was no significant difference in the level of assertiveness in different Caste groups (General, OBC, SC and ST) of teacher-trainees. Null hypothesis was thus accepted in terms of interaction between level of assertiveness and caste group membership for the overall group of female teacher-trainees.

(ii) Income wise groups of female teacher-trainees do not differ on their level of assertiveness.

Test of null hypothesis, specifying no significant difference among the female teacher-trainees belonging to different income groups, was accepted for the overall group of trainees through the findings of present study. In general, the study accepted null hypothesis specifying no significant difference in the level of assertiveness among female teachertrainees belonging to different income groups.

(iii) Groups of female teacher-trainees identified on the basis of occupational background of family do not differ in their level of assertiveness.

This null hypothesis was found to be true for comparisons made across the overall group of teacher-trainees. Null hypothesis-iii was, therefore, accepted for the overall population of female teacher-trainees

(iv) Groups of female teacher-trainees identified on the basis of educational status of parents do not differ in their level of assertiveness.

This null hypothesis was tested in the overall population of female teacher-trainees. It was found that there was no significant difference in the level of assertiveness among overall population of female teacher-trainees belonging to fathers educated to different levels. In general, null hypothesis-iv was accepted for overall population of female teachertrainees.

(v) Academic achievement wise groups of female teacher-trainees do not differ in their level of assertiveness.

This null hypothesis was again found to be true for comparisons made across the overall group of teacher-trainees. Null hypothesis-v was therefore, accepted for overall group of female teacher-trainees.

Hypothesis-2: There is no significant effect of assertiveness training on level of assertiveness of female teacher-trainees.

A test of this hypothesis revealed that at the posttest level there exists significant difference in the level of assertiveness between teachertrainees belonging to control group, which was not given assertiveness training, and the experimental group trainees, who received six days training through a specifically designed assertiveness training programme. Moreover, gain score comparison on the level of assertiveness after intervention revealed significant difference between the control and experimental groups. This indicates that assertiveness training provided to teacher-trainees was significantly effective in increasing level of assertiveness in the experimental group. Null hypothesis was, thus, rejected in terms of effect of assertiveness training on level of assertiveness among female teacher-trainees.

Hypothesis-3: There is no significant effect of assertiveness training on level of self-acceptance of female teacher-trainees.

This hypothesis was tested through comparing posttest and gain scores obtained on dependent variable of self-acceptance of teachertrainees belonging to control and experimental groups. It was found that there exists significant difference between self-acceptance scores of female teacher-trainees belonging to control and experimental groups. The level of self-acceptance was revealed to be significantly higher in case of trainees belonging to experimental group. Test of null hypothesis, specifying no significant effect of assertiveness training on the level of self-acceptance of female teacher- trainees was, thus, rejected through findings of present study.

Hypothesis-4: There is no significant effect of assertiveness training on level of academic achievement motivation of female teacher-trainees.

This null hypothesis was found to be true for comparisons made across posttest scores obtained on academic achievement motivation by teacher-trainees from control and experimental groups. However, significant difference was obtained on gain scores on level of academic achievement motivation between teacher-trainees of control and experimental groups. This, indicated that gain in level of academic achievement motivation was significant in the experimental group trainees.

Thus, it may be stated that the null hypothesis-4 is only partially true.

Hypothesis-5 (i): There is no significant differential effect of assertiveness training on level of assertiveness in groups of female teacher-trainees identified on the basis of caste

A test of this hypothesis revealed no significant difference in level of assertiveness among 'General' and 'Others' caste trainees within the experimental group. This indicates that effect of assertiveness training was similar on assertiveness of both 'General' and 'Others' caste groups. Null hypothesis-5 (i) was, thus, accepted in terms of effect of assertiveness training on level of assertiveness in groups of female teacher-trainees identified on the basis of caste.

Hypothesis-5 (ii): There is no significant differential effect of assertiveness training on level of assertiveness in groups of female teachertrainees identified on the basis of family income.

This hypothesis was tested across subgroups identified within control and experimental subgroups, and revealed no significant difference in assertiveness of female teacher-trainees within experimental subgroups after receiving training. This revealed that assertiveness training was significantly and equally effective in increasing level of assertiveness in experimental subgroups identified on the basis of family income. Null hypothesis-5 (ii) thus found to be true.

Hypothesis-5 (iii): There is no significant differential effect of assertiveness training on level of assertiveness in groups of female teachertrainees identified on the basis of occupational background of family

A test of Null hypothesis-5 (iii) revealed no significant difference in level of assertiveness among trainees belonging to fathers engaged in 'others' and 'service' occupations within control and experimental groups. This indicated that assertiveness training given in experimental group was significantly and similarly effective in increasing level of assertiveness in two groups of teacher-trainees identified within experimental group on the basis of father's occupation. Therefore, Null hypothesis-5 (iii) was accepted for subgroups comparison of female teacher-trainees of experimental group.

Hypothesis-5 (iv): There is no significant differential effect of assertiveness training on level of assertiveness in groups of female teachertrainees identified on the basis of parent's educational status

This hypothesis was tested within subgroups identified in control and experimental groups. Findings related to father's educational status revealed highly significant effect of assertiveness training on level of assertiveness of trainees belonging to fathers either 'illiterate' or educated up to primary level in comparison to trainees belonging to fathers educated higher than primary level. Null hypothesis- 5 (iv) was, thus, rejected for the subgroups comparison within experimental group on the basis of fathers education.

Hypothesis-5 (v): There is no significant differential effect of assertiveness training on level of assertiveness in groups of female teachertrainees identified on the basis of academic achievement

A test of Null hypothesis-5 (v) revealed significant difference within experimental group trainees in terms of assertiveness. Teacher-trainees with 'low' academic achievement were found to have attained significantly higher level of assertiveness than the trainees with 'average and high' academic achievement status. This indicated high significant effect of assertiveness training on assertiveness among trainees with 'low academic achievement' in experimental group. Therefore, Null hypothesis-5 (v) was rejected for subgroups comparison of female teacher-trainees in experimental group.

5.3.0 Conclusions of the Study

In perspective of objectives outlined for the study, findings obtained in the above sections, facilitated derivation of specific conclusions. These conclusions may be stated as follows-

5.3.1 On the basis of findings of present study, it may be concluded that caste group membership, family income, occupation carried out by father, educational status of father and academic achievement factors do not play a significant role in shaping level of assertiveness among female teachertrainees. Mother's educational status, however, tend to be particularly important in this respect, as it influences assertiveness level of female teacher-trainees in a significant way.

5.3.2 The specifically designed assertiveness training programme influences level of assertiveness, self-acceptance and academic achievement motivation among female teacher-trainees at B.Ed.level in a positive manner.

5.3.3 The effect of assertiveness training provided to female teachertrainees during experiment did not vary across teacher-trainees of different caste groups, income groups and father's occupational group. However, assertiveness training was found to differentially affect subgroups based of educational status of father and trainee's academic achievement status. It has been observed that effect of assertiveness training was significantly more positive among trainees belonging to fathers with low educational status and those who had poorer academic achievement.

In general, it may be stated that Assertiveness Training Programme is important for teacher-trainees at B.Ed. level because this tend to enhance their Assertiveness, Self-acceptance and Academic-achievement Motivation. Enhancement of these characteristics is presumed to add to the overall functioning of teacher-trainees as teachers in classrooms.

5.4.0 Implications of the Study

Significant implications for further research in the area could be derived through the findings and conclusions of present study. Direct implications for B.Ed. training programme and policy making, have also been derived. Implications of present study for further research in the area and for the improvement of teacher training programme and policy making are indicated in following subsections.

5.4.1 Implications for Further Research in the Area

Significant effect of assertiveness training on psychological characteristics explored in present study among female teacher-trainees indicates that assertiveness training provided through a specifically designed training programme could facilitate development of similar positive psychological factors. The effect of assertiveness training can be analyzed in terms of various socio-demographic as well as personal characteristics of teacher-trainees. Some of these can be age, gender, nature of residence, type of teacher-training institution, marital status, academic stream, birth order, educational status, nature of family and family size. The search for factors interacting with assertiveness in behaviour needs to be directed towards these and similar 'socio-psychological' dimensions of home environment as well as personal characteristics of teacher-trainees.

The search for the effect of assertiveness training among pre-service and in-service teachers should not remain confined to psychological characteristics of the individuals. Instead, this search should focus attention on variables like mental-health, quality of teaching-learning, teaching behaviours, teacher-pupil relationship, interpersonal relationship in social spheres and classroom management practices in terms of democraticdominating behaviours, degree of openness allowed in classroom situation and attitude towards organizational policies permitting students participation, initiation and expression of feelings and thoughts.

The fact that female teacher-trainees belonging to 'illiterate' mothers tended to be lower in assertiveness indicates that among females level of assertiveness tends to be influenced by mother's educational status in a natural way. A search of 'naturally' existing inhibitory factors within this group need to be undertaken in a more intensive manner.

The findings of present study have revealed significant effect of assertiveness training on level of assertiveness, self–acceptance and academic achievement motivation among female teacher-trainees at B.Ed. level. Factors related to trainee's level of intelligence, attitude and interest towards teaching, facilities available for self-development, presence or absence of conducive environment within family etc. may also have a bearing on level of assertiveness, self-acceptance and academic achievement motivation of trainees. Therefore, evaluation of assertiveness training in terms of effectiveness should be undertaken on a long term basis, through designing follow-up evaluation. All these factors may interact with the effect of assertiveness training on study variables in specific ways, and future research in this area needs to consider pertinent mediating variables, while testing the effect of assertiveness training on level of assertiveness, self-acceptance and academic achievement motivation among participants.

At this stage presence of significant and direct effect of assertiveness training on level of assertiveness, self-acceptance and gain in academic achievement motivation, as obtained in present study, justify the relevance of assertiveness training as a personality development programme in teacher education curriculum. Besides, organization of activities related to different skills with the help of a well-designed programme during teacher training is a need of the hour. The selfenhancement component emphasized in new teacher education curriculum in NCFTE (2010), and proposed NCTE (2014) document, seem to be a step in this direction.

In view of above discussion, following research areas ensue directly from the findings and conclusions of present study-

(a) Study of effect of assertiveness training programme on the classroom behaviours of in-service teachers.

(b) study of effect of assertiveness training programme on teaching effectiveness of in-service teachers.

(c) Study of effect of assertiveness training programme on the improvement of teaching skills of pre-service teachers. .

(d) Study of effect of assertiveness training programme on teacher-pupil relationship of in-service teachers.

(e) Comparative study of effect of assertiveness training programme on the level of assertiveness of in-service teachers at primary and secondary level.

(f) Comparative study of effect of assertiveness training programme on level of assertiveness among students at primary and secondary level.

(g) Study of effect of assertiveness training programme on communication skills of pre-service and in-service teachers.

(h) Study of effect of assertiveness training programme on the social skills of pre-service and in-service teachers.

5.4.2 Implications of Present Study for Classroom Practice and Policy making

Findings of present study indicated positive consequences of assertiveness training on level of assertiveness, self-acceptance and academic achievement motivation among female teacher-trainees. This was also supported by a number of studies. Thus, positive consequences of assertiveness training on trainee's psychological characteristics emphasize that this practice needs to be nurtured through organization of specially designed assertiveness training programmes for benefit of pre-service and in-service teachers as well as students. Lack of organization of assertiveness training programmes in Indian teacher education system highlights the need to introduce such components within the training institutions as well as in the school settings. For this, selected teacher educators within each training institution need to be trained for organizing suitably developed assertiveness development programme. Teacher education policies, needs to be evolved so that, the development of assertiveness among prospective teachers becomes an integral part of teacher-training process.

5.5.0 Limitations of Present Study

The present study was considerably influenced by the limitations of time and resources. The sample was drawn from the teacher-training institutions affiliated to a single university only, which limits the generalizations of findings obtained. The nature of relationship between selected variables could be studied in detail with the use of tools standardized on a more representative sample. The present work included only a limited set of socio-demographic characteristics in the analysis and failed to include certain important socio-psychological variables as causative factors of assertiveness in behaviour. These limitations need to be considered before making any generalization from the study. Still further, the study failed to visualize some intervening variables while testing the effect of assertiveness training on level of assertiveness, selfacceptance and academic achievement motivation among female teachertrainees. These deficiencies, needs to be remove in future research work.

Bibliography

Abed, G.A. et.al. (2015). The Effect of Assertiveness Training Program on Improving Self-Esteem of Psychiatric Nurses. Journal of Nursing Science. Vol.1, No.1, 1-8.

Agbakwuru, C. & U. Stella (2012). Effect of Assertiveness Training on Resilience among Early Adolescents. European Scientific Journal, Vol. 8,No. 10, 69-84.

Akbari, B. et.al. (2012). Effects of Assertiveness Training Methods on Self-Esteem and General Self-Efficacy of Islamic Azad University, Anzali Branch. Journal of Basic and Applied Scientific Research. Vol.2, No.3,2265-2269.

Akinteye, A.J. (2012). Effect of Mentoring and Assertiveness Training on Adolescents' Self-esteem in Lagos State Secondary Schools. Lagos. Unpublished Ph.D. Thesis.

Alberti, R.E. & M.L. Emmons (1974). Your Perfect Right: A Guide for Assertive Living. California: Impact, San Luis Obispo.

Alberti, Robert E., Emmons & L. Michael (1974), Stand up, Speak out, Talk back. Canada Simon and Schuster Ltd. Markhan.

Alden, et. al. (1978). A Comparison of Cognitive and Skills Training Strategies in the Treatment of Unassertive Clients. Behavior Therapy, vol.9, 843-846.

Alberti, R. E. & M. L.Emmons (2008). Your Perfect Right: Assertiveness and Equality in Your Life and Relationships (9th ed.). Atascadero, CA: Impact Publishers.

Anant, H.S. (2009). The Importance and Benefits of Assertiveness Training. Knowledge and Human Development Authority. www.anant.org.com. (Retrieved on 15-03-2011).

Arslan, Esin et.al. (2013). Levels of Assertiveness and Peer Pressure of Nursing Students. International Journal of Caring Sciences. Vol. 6, No. 1, 78-86.

Ashouri, A. et.al. (2008). The Effectiveness of Assertive Training Group Therapy in decreasing Aggression and improving Academic Achievement in High School Students. Journal of Psychiatry and Clinical Psychology. Vol.14, No.4, 389-93.

Asokan, M. & R. Muthumanickan (2013). A Study on Students' Self control in relation to Assertiveness Behaviour. International Journal of Teacher Educational Research. Vol.2, No.1, 36-42.

Asrowi & M. Barida (2013). The Effectiveness of Assertive Training to Increase the Communication Skills of High School Students in Surakarta. DIJE. Vol.1, 95-105.

Averett M., & M. McManis(1977), Relationship between Extraversion and Assertiveness and Related Personality Characteristics. Psychological Reports, 41, 95-96.

Babayi, M.S. & A. Rahmati (2014). Effects of Assertive Training on Social Anxiety of Shahid Bahonar University of Kerman. Reef Resources Assessment and Management Technical Paper. Vol.40, No.3, 295-301.

Barbaree, H.E. & R.B. Davis (1984). Assertive Behavior, Self expectations and Self evaluations in Mildly Depressed University Women, Journal of Cognitive Therapy and Research. Vol. 8, No. 2, 153-171.

Beaver, B.E. (1987). Assertiveness Training: Its Effect upon Academic Achievement and Self-Concept of Vocational Nursing Students. Dissertation Abstract International, Vol. 48, No. 6, 1385.

Beck, J.G. & R.G. Heimberg (1983). Self Report Assessment of Assertive Behavior: A Critical Analysis. Behavior Modification, Vol.7, No.4, 451-487.

Begley, C.M & M. Glacken (2004). Irish Nursing Students' Changing levels of Assertiveness during their Pre-registration Program. Nurse Education Today, Vol. 24, No. 7, 501-510.

Bell, Y.R. & M.K. Jakson, (1984). Assertive Behavior among Black College Students. Journal of Black Psychology, Vol. 11, No. 1, 19-27.

Best,John W., and James V. Kahn (1986), Research in Education. Prentice-Hall of India Pvt. Ltd., New Delhi.

Bishop, S. (2010). Develop Your Assertiveness (2nd ed.). London: Kogan Page.

Booraem, C.D. & J.V. Flowers (1978). A Procedural Model for Training of Assertive Behavior. In J.M. Whiteley & J.V. Flowers (Eds.), Approaches to Assertion Training (15-46). Monetery, CA: BrookdCole.

Branaman, T.F. (1979). Facilitative Anxiety and Assertive Behavior in Academic Achievement of Students. College Student's Journal, Vol. 13, No. 1, 62-64.

Branden, N. (1987). How to Raise Your Self-esteem? New York: Bantam Books.

Branden, N. (1995). The Six Pillars of Self-Esteem. New York: Bantam Books.

Brockway, B.S. (1976). Assertiveness Training for Professional Women. Social Work, Vol. 21, No. 6, 498.

Buell, G. & J. Snyder (1981), Assertiveness Training with Children. Psychological Reports, 49 (1), 71-80.

Butler, P. (1992). Self-Assertion for Women. San Francisco: Harper. Cassel, R.N. & J. Blackwell (2002). Positive Assertiveness begins with Character Education and Includes the Abuse of Cigarettes, Alcohol and Drugs. Journal of Instructional Psychology, Vol. 29, No. 2, 77-79.

Castro, G. (1999). American Feminism: A Contemporary History. New York: University Press.

Chan, D. W. (1993). Components of Assertiveness: Their Relationships with Assertive Rights and Depressed Mood among Chinese College Students in Hong Kong. Behaviour Research and Therapy, 31(5), 529-538.

Chapman, A. (2008). Assertiveness and Self-Confidence: How to Help Build, Boost and Develop Self-Confidence and Assertiveness. Journal of Business Balls Space, Vol. 13, 56-464.

Chaudhary, S.S. (2012). Teacher Education: An Introspection. University News, Vol. 50, No.19, May 07-13, 10-15.

Chiauzzi, E. J. & R.G. Heimberg (1986). Legitimacy of Request and Social Problem Solving: A Study of Assertive and Nonassertive Subjects. Behavior Modification, Vol.10, No. 1, 3-18.

Chibuike, O.B. et.al.(2013). Role of Locus of Control on Assertive Behavior of Adolescents. International Journal of Health and Psychology Research. Vol.1, No.1, 38-44.

Chinwe, O. (2015). Implementation of Assertive Training and Systematic Desensitization in Reducing Examination Phobia among University Students. Journal of Education Research and Behavioral Sciences. Vol.4, No.1, 001-004.

Chitenden, G.E. (1942). An Experimental Study in Measuring and Modifying Assertive Behavior in Young Children. Monographs of the Society for Research in Child Development, Vol.7, 1-87.

Christopher, A., C. Edwards & C. Eppler (2012). School Based Group Counseling. Belmont, CA: Brooks-Cole.

Combes, A.S. (1995), Improving the Confidence of Preadolescent girls by Focusing on the Development of Positive Self esteem, Body image, and Assertiveness skills. Practicum paper. Southeastern University.

Corey, G. (2009). Theory and Practice of Counselling and Psychotherapy. (8th Edition) Thomson Books/ Cole Publishing Coy.

Crandall, R., D.A. McCown & Z. Robb (1988). The Effects of Assertiveness Training on Self-actualization. Small Group Behavior, Vol. 19, No. 1, 134-145.

Crawford, M. (1988). Gender, Age and the Social Evaluation of Assertion. Behavior Modification, Vol.12, No.4, 549-564.

Crassini, B. et. al. (1979). Sex Differences in Assertive Behavior, Australian Journal of Psychology. Vol. 31, No. 1, 15-19.

Delamater, R.J. and J.R. McNamara (1985). Perceptions of Assertiveness by high and Low Assertive Female College Students. The Journal of Psychology, Vol. 119, No. 6, 581-586.

Delamater, R.J. and J.R. McNamara (1986). The Social Impact of Assertiveness: Research Findings and Clinical Implications. Behavior Modification, Vol.10, No.2. 139-158.

Delamater,R.J. and J.R. McNamara (1991). Perceptions of Assertiveness by Women involved in a Conflict Situation. Behavior Modification, Vol.15, No.2, 173-193.

Deltsidu, A. (2009). Undergraduate Nursing Student's level of Assertiveness in Greece: A Questionnaire Survey. Journal of Nurse Education Practice, Vol. 9, No. 5, 322-330.

Deluty, R.H. (1981). Adaptiveness of Aggressive, Assertive and Submissive Behavior for Children. Journal of Clinical Child and Adolescent Psychology, Vol. 10, No. 3. 155-158.

Deluty, R.H. (1979). Children's Action Tendency: A Self Report Measures of Aggressiveness, Assertiveness and Submissiveness in Children. Journal of Consulting and Clinical Psychology, Vol. 47, No. 6, 1061-1071.

Dhoundiyal, N.C. (2005). Assertiveness Skills Training Programme. Unpublished Manuscript. Faculty of Education, Kumaun University Campus, Almora. Dhoundiyal, N.C. (2010), A Qualitative List of Assertive Behaviour for Test Construction, Faculty of Education, Kumaun University Campus, Almora.

Dickson, A. (1982). A Woman in Your Own Right: Assertiveness and You. London: Quartet Books.

Donnelly, G. F. (1992). An Assertiveness Training Program for a group of Elders. Holistic Nursing Practice, Vol. 7, No. 1, 5.

Doty, L. (1987). Communication and Assertion Skills for Older Persons. Washington: Hemisphere Publishing Corporation.

Dura, J.R. and S. Beck (1986). Psychiatric Aides Perceptions of a Patient's Behaviors. Behavior Modification, Vol.10, No.3, 301-314.

Edwards, C. (2005). Classroom Discipline and Management. New York: John Wiley & Sons Inc.

Eisler, R. et. al. (1973). Components of Assertive Behavior. Journal of Clinical Psychology, Vol. 29, No.3, 295-299.

Eisler, R. et. al. (1975). Situational Determinants of Assertive Behavior Journal of Consulting and Clinical Psychology, Vol. 43, 330-340.

Eisler, R. et.al(1978). The Relationship of Cognitive Variables to the Expression of Assertiveness. Behavior Therapy, Vol. 9, 419-427.

Ekundayo, O.S. (2010). Gender, Marital Status and Religious Affiliation as Factors of Assertiveness among Nigerian Education Majors. Journal of Social Science, Vol. 5, No. 6, 467-470.

Eldeeb, G.A. et.al. (2014). Assertiveness and Stress among Undergraduate Nursing Students at Menoufyia University. Vol.4, No.4, 30-37.

Elliot, Timothy R. et al (1991), Personal Assertiveness and the Effects of Social Support among College Students, Psychological Abstracts, 78 (3), 7251.

Entwistle, N.J. (1968), Academic Motivation and School Attainment. British Journal of Educational Psychology, 38 (2) , 181-188.

Epstein, N. (1980). Social Consequences of Assertion, Aggression and Submission: Situational and Dispositional Determinants. Behavior Therapy, Vol. 11, No. 5, 662-669.

Fensterheim, H. (1973), Behavior Therapy: Assertive Training in Groups. The Counseling Psychologist, 5 (4), 20-29.

Fenesterhiem, H.&A.J. Bear (1978),Don't Say 'Yes' when you want to say 'No'. Del Publishing Company, New York.

Fiedler, D. & L.R. Beach (1978). On the Decision to be Assertive. Journal of Consulting and Clinical Psychology, Vol. 46, No. 3, 537-546.

Fenesterhiem, H. and A.J. Bear (1978). Don't Say Yes, When You Want to Say No. Del Publishing Company, New York.

Firth, N. (2001). The Effect of An Assertiveness Training Program on Locus of Control of Students with Specific Learning Difficulties: A Qualitative Case Study. Young Adolescents Research Journal, Vol. 2, No. 1, 15-31.

Florian, V. & E.Z.Shurka (1987). The Effect of Culture and Gender on Self Reported Assertive Behavior, International Journal of Psychology. Vol. 22, No. 1, 83-95.

Flowers, J.V. (2006). Goal Clarity as a Component of Assertive Behavior and a Result of Assertion Training. Journal of Clinical Psychology, Vol. 34, No. 3, 744-747.

Fodor, E.M. et.al. (2006). The Power Motive and Affective Response to Assertiveness. Journal of Research in personality, Vol. 40, 598-610.

Franzke, A. W. (1987). The Effects of Assertiveness Training on older Adults. The Gerontologist, 27(1), 13-16.

Fukuyama, M.A. & T.K.Greenfield (1983). Dimensions of Assertiveness in an Asian-American Student Population. Journal of Counseling Psychology, Vol. 30, No. 3, 429- 432.

Galassi, J.P. et. al. (1974). The College Self Expression Scale: A Measure of Assertiveness. Journal of Behavior Therapy, Vol. 5, 165-171.

Galassi, J.P. & M.D. Galassi (1974). Validity of a Measure of Assertiveness. Journal of Counseling Psychology, Vol. 21, No. 3, 248- 250.

Galassi, J.P. & M.D. Galassi (1979). Relationship between Assertiveness and Factorial Validated. Cognitive Therapy and Research Journal, Vol. 6, 45-52.

Galassi, D. M., M. C. Litz, & J. P. Galassi, (1974). Assertive Training in Groups using Video Feedback. Journal of Counseling Psychology, 21(5), 390-394.

Gangwar, J.P. (2012). Study of The Relationship among Assertive Behavior, Academic Achievement and Level of Participation in Cocurricular Activities of Secondary level Students.

Unpublished Doctoral Dissertation in Education, Kumaun University, Nainital. Gerry, E.M. (1989). An Investigation into the Assertive Behavior of Trained Nurses in General Hospital Settings. Journal of Advanced Nursing, Vol. 14, No.12, 1002-1008.

Gervasio, A.H. and M.Crawford (1989). Social Evaluations of Assertiveness. Psychology of Women Quarterly, Vol. 13, 1-25.

Grant, J. & S. Devorah (1980). Assertiveness Training: A program for High School Students. Journal of School Counselor, Vol. 27, No. 3, 230-237.

Goldberg-Lillehoj and R. Spoth (2005). Assertiveness among Young Rural Adolescents Relationship to Alcohol use. DO1, Vol.10, 39-68.

Goodman, M. & B. Fallon (1995). Pattern Changing for Abused Women: An Educational Program. Thousand Oaks, CA: Sage Publications.

Greco, L.D. et. al. (1981). The Rathus Assertiveness Schedule Modified for Early Adolescents. Journal of Psychology and Behavioral Assessment, Vol. 3, No. 4, 321-328.

Gupta, et. al. (2002). Effects of Different Techniques of Assertiveness Training on Students Self-Concept. Recent Research in Education and Psychology, Vol.7, 19-24.

Gupta, A.S. & Shagufta (2007). Achievement Motivation and Adjustment Patterns. A Comparative View of Visually Disabled and Normal Pupils. Praachi Journal of Psycho-Cultural Dimensions. Vol.23, No.1, 14-18.

Giivena, M. (2010). An Analysis of the Vocational Education Undergraduate Student's levels of Assertiveness and Problem Solving skills. Procedia, Journal of Social and Behavioral Science, Vol. 2, No. 2, 2064-2070.

Haladin, N.B. et.al. (2013). Assertiveness among Undergraduates in a Malaysian Public University: Implications Towards improved Employability. Jurnal Teknologi (Social Sciences). Vol.65, No.2, 15-24.

Hasanzadeh, R. & G. Mahdinejad (2012). Investigation of the Relationship between Self-assertiveness and Schools' attitude. Journal of Elementary Education. Vol.22, No.1, 81-88.

Hashemi, F. (2007). Effects of Self Expression Training on Guidance School Female Students' Happiness in Rey City.

Unpublished M.Sc.Thesis. Training Science Department, Allameh Tabatabaei University.

Hatzenbuehler, L.C. & H.E. Schroeder (1982). Assertiveness Training with Outpatients : The Effectiveness of Skills and Cognitive Procedures. Journal of Behavioral Psychotherapy, Vol. 10, No. 3, 234-252.

Hedrick, T.E. & J.E. Chance (1977). Sex Differences in Assertive Achievement Patterns. Journal of Behavioral Science Sex Roles, Vol. 3, No. 2, 129-139.

Heighway, S., S. Webster & S. Webster (1992). S.T.A.R.S.: Skills Training for Assertiveness, Relationship-Building, and Sexual Awareness. Madison, WI: Wisconsin Council on Developmental Disabilities.

Heimberg, R.G. et. al. (1983). Cognitive Mediation of Assertive Behavior: An Analysis of Self Statement Patterns of College Students, Psychiatric

Patients and Normal Adults. Journal of Cognitive Therapy and Research, Vol. 7, No. 5, 455-463.

Heimberg, R.G. & R.E. Becker (1981). Cognitive and Behavioral Models of Assertive Behavior: Review Analysis and Integration. Clinical Psychology Review, Vol. 1, No. 3, 353-373.

Hernandez, S.K. and P.A. Mauger (1980). Assertiveness, Aggressiveness and Eysenk's Personality Variables. Journal of Personality and Individual Differences, Vol.1, No.2, 143-149.

Herni, R.M. & M. Fakhrurrozzi (2007). Relationship between Assertive Behavior with Confidence for College Students. http://www.gunaderma.ac.id.com. (Retrieved on 15.03.2011).

Herzberger, S.D., et.al (1984). The Development of An Assertiveness Self-Report Inventory. Journal of Personality Assessment, Vol. 48, No. 3, 317- 323.

Hobbs, S.A. & D.L.Walle (1985). Validation of Children's Assertive Behavior Scale. Journal of Psychopathology and Behavioral Assessment, Vol. 7, No. 2, 145-153.

Hoffman, D. H. (1983). Assertion training: A tool for teacher educators. Ilinois: Harper.

Hollandsworth, J.G. & K.E. Wall (1977). Sex Differences in Assertive Behavior : An Empirical Investigation. Journal of Counseling Psychology, Vol. 24, 217-222.

Hwang, Y.S., C. Echols & K. Vrongistions (2002), Multidimensional Academic Motivation of High Achieving African American students .College Student Journal, 36 (4),544-554.

Ibrahim, C. (2015). An Investigation of High school Seniors' Assertiveness levels based on their Demographic Characteristics. Educational Research and Reviews. Vol.10, No.5, 615-621.

Ibrahim, S.A. (2011). Factors Affecting Assertiveness among Student Nurses. Journal of Education Today, Vol. 31, No. 4, 356-360.

Iruloh, B.N. & G.N. Amadi (2008). Psychological Perspective of Drug Abuse, prevention and Treatment, University of Port Harcourt Press, Port Harcourt, Nigeria.

Jakubowski-Spector, P. (1973). Facilitating the Growth of Women Through Assertive Training. The Counseling Psychologist, 4(1), 75-86.

Joiner, J.G. et. al. (1982). Evaluation of Assertiveness of Disabled Persons in the Rehabilitation Process. Rehabilitation Counseling in Bulletin, Vol. 26, No. 1, 55-58.

Kakkar,S.B (2010),Self Acceptance Inventory. Catalogue, National Psychological Corporation, Agra.

Kim, Y. (2003). The Effect of Assertiveness Training on Enhancing the Social Skills of Adolescents with Visual impairments. Journal of Visual Impairment and Blindness, Vol. 97, No. 5, 285-297.

Karagozoglu, S. et. al. (2007). Self-esteem and Assertiveness of Final Year Turkish University Students. Nurse Education Today, Vol. 28, No. 5, 641-649.

Kashani, P.A. & M. Bayat (2010). The Effect of Social Skills Assertiveness Training on Assertiveness and Self-esteem Increase of 9-11year old Female Students in Tehran, Iran. World Applied Science Journal, Vol. 9, No. 9, 1028-1032.

Kaufman, C., L., Raphael & P. Espeland (2000). A Teacher's Guide to Stick up for Yourself: A 10-part Course in Self-esteem and Assertiveness for Kids. Minneapolis, MN: Free Spirit Publishing Inc.

Kaur,T.& M. Mehta (2007), Effects of Assertiveness and Self Confidence upon Patterns of Reaction To Frustration and Adjustment. Praachi Journal of Psycho Cultural. Dimensions, Vol.23, No. (1), 83-91.

Kazdin, A.E. & S. Mascitelli (1982). Behavioral Rehearsal, Selfinstructions and Homework practice in developing Assertiveness. Behavior Therapy, Vol. 13, No. 3, 346-360.

Kazdin, A.E. & S. Mascitelli (1982). Covert and Overt rehearsal and Homework practice in developing Assertiveness. Journal of Consulting and Clinical Psychology, Vol. 50, No. 2, 250-258.

Kazdin, A.E. (1982). The Separate and Combined effects of Covert and Overt Rehearsal in developing Assertive Behavior. Journal of Behavior Research Therapy, Vol. 20, No. 1, 17-25.

Kean, T.M. et. al. (1990). Assessing Subjective Responses to Assertive Behavior. Journal of Behavior Modification, Vol. 14, No. 1, 21-36.

Kean, T.M. et.al. (1983). Black's Perceptions of Assertive Behavior: An Empirical. Behavior Modification, Vol.7, No.1, 97-111.

Kearney, P. et. al. (1984). Factors analysis of the Rathus Assertiveness Schedule and the Personal report of Communication Apprehension-24: Replication and Extension. Psychological Report, Vol. 54, 851-854.

Kelley, C. (1979). Assertion training: A Facilitator's Guide. San Diego, CA: University Associates.

Kelly, J.A., et. al. (1980). Reactions to Assertive versus Unassertive Behavior: Differential Effects for Males and Females and Implications for Assertiveness Training. Journal of Behavior Therapy, Vol. 11, No. 5, 670- 682.

Kern, J.M. & R.J. Paquette (1992). Reactions to Assertion in "Controlled" Naturalistic Relationships: Perceptions of Likability and Competency.

Behavior Modification, Vol.16, No.3, 371-386.

Kilkus, S.P. (1993). Assertiveness among Professional Nurses. Journal of Advanced Nursing, Vol. 18, No. 8, 1324-1330.

Kimble, C.E. et. al. (1984). Sex, Age and Cultural differences in Selfreported Assertiveness. Psychological Reports, 55, 419-422.

Landazabal, M.G. (1999). Assessment of a Co-operative Creative Program of Assertive Behavior and Self concept. The Spanish Journal of Psychology, Vol. 2, No. 1, 3-10.

Lange, A.J. & P. Jacubowski (1976). Responsible Assertive Behavior. Illinois: Research Press Champaign. Lavin, J. (1990). A Study to determine the Relationship between Assertiveness and Self-esteem, Conflict Management Style and other selected variables in Female Registered Nurses. Gottesman Library Archieve, Unpublished Historical Dissertation.

Lazarus, A. (1971). Behavior Therapy and Beyond. New York: McGraw-Hill.

Lazarus, A. (1973). On Assertive Behavior: A Brief Note. Behavior Therapy, 4(5), 697-699.

Lazarus, S. Richard (1971), Adjustment and Personality, New York, Holt Rinenart Winston.

Lee, S. & M.S. Crockett (1994). Effect of Assertiveness Training on Levels of Stress and Assertiveness experienced by Nurses in Taiwan, Republic of China. Journal of Issues in Mental Health Nursing, Vol. 15, No. 4, 419-432.

Leman, K. (1998). Women Who Try Too Hard: Breaking the Pleaser Habits. Ada, MI: Revell.

Levin, R.B. and A.M. Gross (1984). Reactions to Assertive versus Nonassertive Behavior. Behavior Modification, Vol. 8, No. 4, 581-592.

Levin, R.B. and A.M. Gross (1987). Assertiveness style: Effects on Perceptions of Assertive Behavior. Behavior Modification, Vol. 11, No. 2, 229-242.

Lewinsohn et.al. (1980). Social Competence and Depression. The Role ofI llusory Self-perceptions? Journal of Abnormal Psychology, Vol. 89, 213-219.

Lin, Y. et.al.(2004). Evaluation of an Assertiveness Training Programme on Nursing and Medical Students' Assertiveness, Self-esteem, and Interpersonal Communication Satisfaction. Nurse Education Today. Vol. 24, 656.

Lina, Y.R. et. al. (2004). Evaluation of An Assertiveness Training Program on Nursing and Medical students' Assertiveness, Self-esteem and Interpersonal Communication Satisfaction. Journal of Psychology in the School, Vol. 24, No. 8, 656-665.

Lineberger, M.H. & K.S. Calhoun (1983). Assertive Behavior in Black and White American Undergraduates. The Journal of Psychology, Vol. 113, No. 1,139-148.

Lizarrage, et. al. (2003). Enhancement of Self regulation, Assertiveness and Empathy. Learning and Instruction, Vol. 3, 423-439.

Lobel, T.E. (1981). Personality Correlates of Assertive Behavior. Journal of Personality and Individual Differences. Vol.2, No.3, 252-254.

Lohr, J.M. et.al. (1984). The Relationship of Assertive Behavior in Women and a validated measure of Irrational Beliefs. Cognitive Therapy and Research, Vol. 8, No.3, 287-297.

Lowe, M.R. & M.A. Storm (1986). Being Assertive or Being Liked: A Genuine Dilemma. Behavior Modification, Vol. 10, No. 4, 371-390

Makhija, M. & P. Singh (2010). Effectiveness of Assertiveness Training Programme on Self Esteem & Academic Achievement in Adolescents. International Research Journal. Vol. I, No. 11, 56-58.

Makhija, M. & P. Singh (2011). The Emotional Factors Which Inhibit or Enhance Assertiveness. Indian Journal of Psychometry and Education.Vol.42,No.2, 176-179.

Makinde,B.O. & A.J.Akinteye (2014). Effects of Mentoring and Assertiveness Training on Adolescents' Self-Esteem in Lagos State Secondary Schools. International Journal of Social Science Studies. Vol.2, No.3, 78-88.

Mansur M.S. (2007). The Effect of Life Skills Training on Progressive Motivation, Self-respecting and Social adaptation. Thought and Behavior in Clinical Psychology.Vol.2, No.6, 85-99.

Marshall, P.G. et. al.(1981). Anxiety reduction, Assertive Training and Enactment of Consequences: A Comparative Study in the Modifications of Non-assertion and Social Fear. Behavior Modification, Vol. 5, No. 1 85-102

McCartan, P. (2006). Assessing Assertive Behavior in Student Nurses: A Comparison of Assertion Measures. Journal of Advanced Nursing, Vol. 15, No. 12, 1370-1376.

Mc Clelland, D.C.et.al. (1953). The Achievement Motive. New York: Appleton-Century-Crafts.

Mcfall, M.E. et. al. (1982). Nonverbal Components in the Communication of Assertiveness. Behavior Modification, Vol. 6, No.1, 121-140

Mentes, A. (2007). The Effect of Sport on High school Student's Assertiveness level. www.futura-technopole.com. (Retrieved on 14.03.2011).

Michelson, L. and R.Wood (1981). Development and Psychometric Properties of Children's Assertive scale. Journal of Psychology and Behavioral Assessment, Vol. 4, No. 1, 3-13.

Monroe, A.B. et. al. (1981). Effects of Conceptual Complexity on Assertive Behavior. Journal of Counseling Psychology, Vol. 28, No. 5, 377-385.

Moon, J. (2009). Achieving Success through Academic Assertiveness: Real Life Strategies for Today's Students. ISBN: 978-0-415-99143-8, Paperback-978-0-415-99142-1.

Mousa, A.A. et.al. (2011). The Effect of an Assertiveness Training Program on Assertiveness Skills and Social Interaction Anxiety of Individuals with Schizophrenia. Journal of American Science. Vol.7, No.12, 454-466.

Mueen, B. et. al. (2006). Relationship of Depression and Assertiveness in Normal Population and Depressed Individuals. Journal of Medical Update, Vol. 1, No. 2. 10-17.

NCTE (2014). Gazzette. www.ncte-india.org/Regulation 2014.pdf. Retrieved on 15.05.2015.

NCFTE (2010). National Curriculum Framework for Teacher Education. www.azimpremjifoundation.org/pdf/NCFTE-2010.pdf. Retrieved on 15.05.2015

Nelsen, E. D. J., R. Duffy, L. Escobar, J. Nelsen, K. Ortolano, & D. Owen-Sohocki, (2001). Positive Discipline: A Teacher's A-Z guide: Hundreds of Solutions for Every Possible Classroom. New York: Three Rivers Press.

Niikura, R. (1986), The Psychological Process Underlying Japanese Assertive Behaviour: Comparison of Japanese with Americans, and Filipinos. Child and Family Behaviour Therapy, Vol.7, No.3, 731-737.

Niusha, B. et.al. (2012). Effects of Assertiveness Training on Test Anxiety of Girl students in First Grade of Guidance School. Procedia-Social and Behavioral Sciences. Vol.46, 1385-1389.

Nnodum, B.I. (2010). Relative Effectiveness of Assertive Training, Modeling and their combination in the Reduction of Isolate Behavior. Edo Journal of Counseling, Vol. 3, No. 1, 1-15.

Noghabaee, M.S. & M. Nikoogoftar (2014). The Effect of Assertiveness Training on Self-efficacy among Iranian High school Female Students. European Online Journal of Natural and Social Sciences. Vol.3, No.1, 123-127.

Nota, L. & S. Soresi (2003), An Assertiveness Training Program for Indecisive Students Attending an Italian University. Career Development Quarterly, Vol. 51, No.4 , 322-334.

Norton, R. & B.Warnick (1976). Assertiveness as a Communication Construct. The Journal of Personality and Individual Differences, Vol. 3, No. 1, 62-66.

Noushad, P.P. and M.A. Musthafa (2008). The Ability to Say 'Yes' or 'No': A Survey on Assertiveness among Secondary School Students. The Journal of Experiments in Education, Vol. 38, No. 1, 1-6.

Okoli, C.E. (2002). Techniques of Behaviour Modification. Lagos. Behenu Press and Publishers.

Onyeizugbo, E.U. (2003). Effects of Gender, Age and Education on Assertiveness in a Nigerian sample. Psychology of Women Quarterly, Vol. 27, No. 1, 12-16.

Orenstein, H. et. al. (1975). Assertiveness and Anxiety: A Correlational Study. Journal of Behavior Therapy and Experimental Psychiatry, Vol. 6, No. 3,203-207.

Orr, K.S. & S.H. Ochoa (2004). College Students Comfort with Assertive Behavior: An Analysis of Students With and Without Disabilities in three different Post-secondary Institutions. Unpublished Doctoral Dissertation, Texas A & M University.

Paeezy, M. et. al. (2010). Investigating the impact of Assertiveness Training on Assertiveness, Subjective well-being and Academic Achievement of Iranian Female Secondary Students. Procedia Social and Behavioral Sciences, Vol. 5, 1447-1450.

Patera, A. & A. Politynou (2008). Observations on Assertiveness and its Relation to Empathy in Greek Students. The Journal of Psychiatrike, Vol. 19, No. 3, 238-244.

Patri, K. & S. Nanda (2011). Attitude of Pupil Teachers Towards Distance Education Programme in Orissa. University News, Vol. 49, No. 28, July 11-17, 9-13.

Pattenson, L. & J. Burns (1990). Women, Assertiveness, and Health: A Rationale for the Use of Training in Promoting Women's Health. London: Health Education Authority.

Peneva, I. & S. Mavrodiev (2013). A Historical Approach to Assertiveness. Psychological Thought. Vol. 6, No. 1, 3-26.

Piccinin, S. et. al. (1998). Impact of Situational Legitimacy and Assertiveness related Anxiety / Discomfort on Motivation and Ability to Generate Effective Criticism Responses. The Journal of Current Psychology, Vol. 17, No.1, 75-92.

Piggrem, G.W. (1980). Life Satisfaction and Assertive Behavior in the Elderly. www.rade.ohiolink edu.com. (Retrieved on 27.04.2011), p-77.

Doc. No. osu-1100789634

Pitcher, S.W. & S. Meikle, (1980). The Topography of Assertive Behavior in Positive and Negative Situations. The Journal of Behavior Therapy, Vol. 11, No. 4, 532-547.

Pitt, A. & B.R. Roth (1978). A Model for Assertive Training: Integration of Feelings and Behavior. Journal of Clinical Social Work, Vol. 6, No. 4, 274-292.

Poyrazli, S. et. al. (2002). Relation between Assertiveness, Academic Self Efficacy and Psychosocial Adjustment among International Graduate Students. The Journal of College Student Development, Vol. 43, No. 5, 632-642.

Rathus, S.A. (1973). A 30-item Schedule for Assessing Assertive Behavior. Behavior Therapy, 4 , 398-406

Rathus, S.A. & J.S. Nevid (1977). Concurrent Validity of the 30-item Assertiveness Schedule with a Psychiatric Population. Journal of Behavior Therapy, Vol. 8, No. 3, 393-397.

Rees, S. & R. S. Graham (1991). Assertion Training: How to be who you really are? New York: Routledge.

Rezan, A. et. al. (2009). The Effectiveness of an Assertiveness Training Program on Adolescent's Assertiveness Level. Journal of Elementary Education, Vol. 8, No. 2, 485-492.

Rich, A.R. & H.E. Schroeder (1976). Research Issues in Assertiveness Training. Psychological Bulletin, Vol. 83, No. 6, 1081-1096.

Robinson, W.L. & K.S. Calhoun (1984). Assertiveness and Cognitive Processing in Interpersonal Situations. Journal of Psychopathology and Behavioral Assessment, Vol.6, No.1, 81-96.

Rodriquez, G.et.al. (2001). Significant Variables associated with Assertiveness among Hispanic College Women. Journal of Instructional Psychology, Vol. 28, No. 3, 184-190.

Rose J.Y. and W.W. Tryon (1979). Judgment of Assertive Behavior as a Function of Speech loudness, Latency, Content, Gestures, Inflection and Sex. Behavior modification, vol. 3 No. 1, 112-123.

Rotheram, M.J. et. al. (1982). Assertiveness Training in Fourth and Fifth grade Children. American Journal of Psychology, Vol.10, No. 5, 567-582.

Rotheram, M.J. & M. Armstrong (1980). Assertiveness Training with High School Students. Journal of Adolescence, Vol. 15, No. 58, 267-276.

Rymbai, B.B. (2011). Need for Professionalism in Higher Education Teachers. University News, Vol. 49, No. 25, June 20-26, 03-10.

Salter, A. (1949). Conditioned Reflex Therapy. New York: Capricorn.
Savage, T., & M. Savage (2010). Successful Classroom Management and Discipline: Teaching Self-control and Responsibility. Thousand Oaks, CA: Sage Publications.

Scherbarth, A. (2002). Assertiveness and Misconceptions of Assertion. Undergraduate Research Journal for the Human Sciences, vol. 1.

Schroeder, H.E. et. al.(1983). The Social Perception of Assertive Behavior as a function of Response, Class and Gender. The Journal of Behavior Therapy, Vol. 14, No. 4, 534-544.

Segal, D.L. (2005). Relationship of Assertiveness, Depression and Social Support among Older Nursing Home Residents. Behavior Modification, Vol. 29, No. 4, 689-9-695.

Sert, A.G. (2003). The Effect of Assertiveness Training on the Assertiveness and Self-esteem level of 5th grade Children. Unpublished Doctoral Dissertation, The Graduate school of Social Science of Middle East Technical University. www.etd.lib.metu.edu.tr. (Retrieved on 14.03.2011).

Sharma,T.R. (2010), Academic Achievement Motivation Test. Catalogue, National Psychological Corporation, Agra.

Shaevitz, M. (1999). The Confident Woman: Learn the Rules of the Game. New York: Harmony Books.

Shepard, L.A. (1978). Self-Acceptance: The Evaluative Component of the Self-concept Construct. American Educational Research Journal. Vol. 16, No. 2, 139-160.

Shepherd, R. (2006). Volitional Strategies and Social Anxiety among College Student. College Quarterly, Vol.9, No. 4.

Shimizu,T., S. Kubota, N. Mishima & S. Nagata (2009), Relationship between Self esteem and Assertiveness Training Among Japanese Hospital Nurses. Elementary Education Online, 8(2), 485-492 Singleton, W.T. (1983). Social Skills. Boston: M.T.P.

Smith, M. J. (1985). When I Say No, I Feel Guilty. New York: Bantam Books.

Stake, J.E., C.J. Deville & C.L. Pennell (1983), The Effects of Assertive Training on the Performance and Self- esteem of Adolescent Girls. Journal of Youth and Adolescence. Vol. 12, 435-440

Stake, Jayne De Ville J. et al (1985), Modelling Parents Assertiveness, Psychological abstracts, 73, 27201.

Stake, E.J., et. al.(2005). The Effect of Assertiveness Training on Performance Self-esteem of Adolescent girls. Netherlands: Springer Stake, J. E., & J. Pearlman (1980). Assertiveness Training as An Intervention Technique for Low Performance Self-esteem Women. Journal of Counseling Psychology, 27 (3), 276-281.

Starke, M.C. (1987). Enhancing Social Skills and Self perceptions of Physically disabled Young Adults: Assertiveness Training versus Discussion Groups. Behavior Modification, Vol. 11, No.1, 3-16.

Stewart, C.G. & W.A. Lewis (1986). Effect of Assertiveness Training on the Self-esteem of Black High school Students. The Journal of Counseling and Development, Vol. 64, No. 10, 638-641.

Sue, D. et. al. (1990). Assertiveness and Social Anxiety in Chinese American Women. Journal of Psychology, Vol. 124, No. 2, 155.

Tanner, V.L. & W.B. Holliman(1988). Effectiveness of Assertiveness Training in Modifying Aggressive Behaviors of Young Children. Psychological Reports, 62 (1), 39-46.

Tannous, F.G. (2015). The Effectiveness of Assertiveness Training in improving Self-esteem among a Sample of Students with Low Emotional- Behavioral Traits. International Journal of Adult and Non Formal Education. Vol.3, No.1, 055-061.

Tavakoli, P. et.al. (2014). The Influence of Assertiveness Training on Selfesteem in Female Students of Government High-schools of Shiraz,

Iran: A Randomized Controlled Trial. Nursing Practice Today. Vol.1, No.1, 17-23.

Tavakoli, S. et. al. (2009). Effect of Assertiveness Training and Expressive writing on Acculturative Stress in International Students: A Randomized Trial. Journal of Counseling Psychology, Vol. 56, No. 4, 590-596.

Thφft, J. S. (1977). Developing Assertiveness in Children. In R. E. Alberti (Ed.), Assertiveness: Innovations, Applications, Issues. San Luis Obispo, CA: Impact.

Thilagavathy, T. (2013). Adjustment and Emotional Intelligence of High School Teachers in Tiruvarur District. International Journal of Teacher Educational Research (IJTER) Vol.2 No.5, 1-6.

Victor, S. & P.M. Lewinsohn (1980). Assertive Behavior and Depression Journal of Consulting and Clinical Psychology, Vol.48, No.1. 119-120.

Williams, J.M. & J.K. Stout (1984), The Effect of High and Low Assertiveness on Locus of Control and Health Problems. Journal of Psychology, 119(2), 169-173.

Wolpe and Lazarus (1966), Defining Assertive Behavior. Psychological Bulletin, 83, 1081- 1096

Weigel, R.M., (2006). Demographic Factors Affecting Assertive and Defensive Behavior in Preschool Children: An Ethological Study. Journal of Aggressive Behavior, Vol. 11, No. 1, 27-40.

Westefeld, J.S. et. al. (1980). Effects of Role playing Instructions on Assertive Behavior: A Methodological Study. Behavior Therapy, Vol. 11, No. 2, 271-277.

Wildman, B.G. and B. Clementze (1986). Assertive, Empathic Assertive and Conversational Behavior: Perception of Likability, Effectiveness and Sex-role. Behavior Modification, Vol. 10, No.3, 315-331.

Wojnilower, D.A. & A.M. Gross (1984). Assertive Behavior and Likeability in Elementary school Boys. Child and Family Behavior Therapy, Vol. 6, No. 4, 57-70.

Wolpe, J. (1958). Psychotherapy by Reciprocal Inhibition. California: Stanford University Press.

Wolpe, J. (1990). The Practice of Behavior Therapy (4th ed.). New York: Pergamon.

Worell, J. (2001). Sex Similarities and Differences: Who are more Assertive in Behavior: Male or Female? Encyclopedia of Women and Gender, Vol. 1, 1-1256.

Xavier Alphonse, SJ (2012). Teaching: A Business or Mission. University News. Vol. 50, No. 36, Sept 03-09, 9-11.

Yong, F.L. (2010). A Study on the Assertiveness and Academic Procrastination of English and Communication Students at a Private University. American Journal of Scientific Research, ISSN-1450-223x,No. 9, 62-75.

Yoshioka, M. (2000). Sustentative Difference in the Assertiveness of Lowincome

African-American, Hispanic and Caucasian Women. The Journal of Psychology, Vol. 134, No. 3, 243-259.

Yusefi,V. et.al. (2015). The Efficacy of The Teaching Group Method Self-Assertiveness Skills on Blind Students Self-esteem. Indian Journal of Fundamental and Applied Life Sciences. Vol.5 (SI), 200-206.

Zade, M.H. et.al. (2009). Effect of Group Assertive Training on Social anxiety, Social skills and Academic performance of Female Students. Behavioral Science. No.1, 59-64.

Zuker, E. (1983). Mastering Assertiveness Skills. New York: Amacom.

Index